THE *'Peyton Place'* MURDER

The True Crime Story Behind The Novel That Shocked The Nation

Renee Mallett

WildBluePress.com

THE 'PEYTON PLACE' MURDER published by:
WILDBLUE PRESS
P.O. Box 102440
Denver, Colorado 80250

Publisher Disclaimer: Any opinions, statements of fact or fiction, descriptions, dialogue, and citations found in this book were provided by the author, and are solely those of the author. The publisher makes no claim as to their veracity or accuracy, and assumes no liability for the content.

ISBN 978-1-952225-62-8 Trade Paperback
ISBN 978-1-952225-61-1 eBook

Interior Formatting/Cover Design by Elijah Toten
www.totencreative.com

THE *'Peyton Place'* MURDER

Table of Contents

Dedication

This book is for Robin, who gave me a place of respite when I didn't know I needed it the most, and because she always makes me laugh.

Introduction

It's an odd book to come from the typewriter of a plump, 32-year-old mother of three children. But Mrs. Metalious is no ordinary housewife.
— Hal Boyle, August 29, 1956

The first time I ever visited the grave of *Peyton Place* author Grace Metalious it was to take pictures for my book *Wicked New Hampshire* (2020, The History Press). The book was a look at all of the more scandalous bits of the Granite State's history— the odd, the quirky, and the little bit criminal. Tucked into a chapter all its own, between centuries-old murders and the like, was a brief recount of the wild life and times of *Peyton Place* author Grace Metalious. Her uniquely New Hampshire upbringing, and certainly her eyebrow-raising bestselling book, seemed like a perfect addition to my own book.

It had been repeated often in news articles and websites that before she died Grace Metalious had used some of that *Peyton Place* payout to buy her own plot in the Smith Meeting House Cemetery in Gilmanton, New Hampshire. To be more precise, the stories said that Grace had bought herself a plot and that she had then bought all of the plots around it so she wouldn't end up, in death, crowded by the neighbors who detested her in life. Another popular tale told about her gravesite was that readers left coins on her simple headstone as a mark of respect for the author.

I didn't expect either of these things to be true.

Wicked New Hampshire was far from my first book. I have spent a good chunk of my adult life chronicling the local legends, lore, and ghost stories of the New England states. It's an offbeat but agreeable kind of work, but it leaves a girl more than just a little jaded. I had also heard that, after she got rich writing, Grace would scandalize the town by roaming around wearing a fur coat— with nothing on underneath. Just as the "let them eat cake!" anecdote had been used against several women in the French nobility before becoming interminably attached to Marie Antoinette, the scandalous naked woman in a fancy coat story has been told about several different New Hampshire women. It was just oddly specific enough that you knew it couldn't be true about *all* of them; the state just wasn't big enough or populated enough to justify these mobs of hypersexualized nouveau riche. In my time collecting local New England myths, I couldn't even count how many stories I'd heard about a cemetery that always *this*, or a graveyard that always *that*. I can much more easily count how many times I've come across the this's and the that's. Because it had happened exactly zero times. Add in the apocryphal stories that were known to always have swirled around (and sometimes been promoted by) Grace, then add in the age of the book that made her famous . . . and, well, it was sure to be a lovely bit of fiction to share in a book of folklore, but it was not anything I really had any faith in. It was exactly the sort of story I came across often when I was researching my books, and those stories always ended up being cut from the whole cloth.

It was an especially fine day the afternoon I drove out to the cemetery in Gilmanton. Late summer, bright sun, but with none of the humidity or heat that New Hampshire's summers are increasingly becoming known for. I drove down a series of roads, each one more backroad than the one before it, surrounded by lush green forests with no houses or signs of life to mar my solitude. New Hampshire is a gorgeous place to live and, if you're not the anxious type that worries about breaking down or running out of gas, it is a beautiful place to wander. As the paved streets turned to dirt and back to asphalt again, I figured my GPS could be letting me down. But it didn't seem to matter all that much. I had the top down on my little red MINI Cooper convertible, hair tied casually back in the same sort of ponytail Grace Metalious had always been known for, and was driving just slow enough to really admire the increasingly rural landscape I was traveling through. It was the perfect day to get a little bit lost and sing along with the radio, with my camera and notebooks thrown haphazardly on the passenger seat next to me.

I was surprised when the woods suddenly parted and I saw a large black gate framing the entrance to Smith Meeting House Cemetery. It was bigger than I had been led to suspect and more modern. I had heard that the oldest headstones dated back to the Revolutionary War and had been expecting more of a collection of jumbled together, broken stones rather than an actual cemetery with carefully trimmed grass and drivable roadways. I doubted even more that I would find Grace's grave. I didn't know the exact location, just a vague direction, and the cemetery spun off far into the distance, dotted with tombstones and trees. I was astonished to not only find the grave very easily but to see that it was set, at least somewhat, further away from its neighbors on all sides. Grace was surprising me right from the start.

I left the car door open behind me as I trekked over to the gravesite, as I always have a paranoid vision of somehow locking my keys in the car in the middle of a cemetery in the middle of nowhere. It's a strange consequence of spending so many years writing ghost stories, I think. The radio played lightly from the car behind me, but low enough that I could still hear birds whistling from the trees. The tombstone was a simple solid block of white, darkened here and there with time, with "Metalious" in large letters above the author's first name and the dates of her birth and death. Camera clutched in one hand I suddenly broke out in laughter. Grace was officially two for two. The grave *was* set apart from the rest of the cemetery residents and the top of the stone was indeed speckled with the very coins I doubted I would see.

There weren't many. Just four or five of them, all different denominations, but one was even a British pound. I clicked off a few pictures of them from a couple of different angles, making sure I got the Metalious name in the shot with the coins, before walking back to my car. One picture down for *Wicked New Hampshire*, thirty-five or so left to go. I wondered if my luck would hold, if I'd be able to find the cottage Aleister Crowley had stayed at one strange summer near Lake Winnipesaukee or if the light wouldn't last and I'd have to make a second trip the next weekend. As I passed by the final resting place of Grace Metalious I reached out with one hand, almost superstitiously, and lightly tapped the top of the stone. One, two, three. Then I dutifully trudged back to my car, felt around under the seats, and found one lone dime hiding along with what seemed like a bucketful of ocean sand and nearly as many desiccated French fries. I reminded myself to vacuum out the car when I got home (spoiler alert: I did not) and walked back to the grave. I carefully placed my dime amid the other offerings, swirling the coins around lightly with one finger, and went on my merry way.

My mother, visiting from New York, was washing dishes when I come home many hours later.

"How'd it go?" she asked. "Get your pictures?"

I told her excitedly about going to Metalious' grave and how, so many years after the publication of *Peyton Place,* there were still coins being left on top. Overall, my mom was not as impressed as I had been.

"Come on," I said. "That's pretty good for someone who *really* only had one book."

"Sometimes all you need is one book," she said. "Look at Harper Lee."

Even outside the horror many readers would feel knowing *To Kill a Mockingbird* had been placed in the same light at *Peyton Place*, the exchange had another problem. I had said *Peyton Place* was Grace Metalious' only book. This was not true. Grace Metalious wrote three more books after her runaway bestselling debut novel that shocked a nation. The year 1959 saw the release of *Return to Peyton Place*, followed by *The Tight White Collar* in 1961, and *No Adam in Eden* in 1963. The three books all sold well enough, but they never struck lightning the way that *Peyton Place* had. Many people are unaware that those three books ever existed, even if *Return to Peyton Place* sold four million copies in paperback. It had even been turned into a movie . . . one *The New York Times* called "so labored, so repetitious of its predecessor (both literally and in terms of more of the same) that it can scarcely reward even the thrill-seeker."[1]

"When did that book come out? *Peyton Place*. Nineteen-sixties?" my mother, an avid reader, asked.

"Nineteen-fifties," I told her, "the TV series was the sixties." Then I asked her if she had ever read it. She said no . . . but she hesitated, for the slightest split second, before she said it. For just the briefest of moments, I saw her about to tell the lie and say that of course she had. Because *Peyton Place*, sixty-four years after being published, has become one those books that everyone has heard so much about they feel like they simply must have read it at some point or another. The TV show and the movie, which earned the modern-day equivalent of $100 million for Fox, further muddy the waters. Had one seen the movie? Or read the book? Or do they just know the plot so well because, for a time, it was the book absolutely everyone was talking about?

My conversation with my mother piqued my curiosity. Over the next few weeks, I casually worked the question into conversations with my librarian friends. Was *Peyton Place* still making the rounds at all among their patrons? Many told me their library had no copies of the book at all. Several didn't have the book but they did have the movie or the five-disc DVD set that made up the full run of the television series. Many of the librarians I knew told me that they had some books about *Peyton Place* but not the novel itself. College libraries seemed to be most likely to still have copies on the shelves. It was quite different from the book's release when it was estimated that one in every twenty-nine Americans owned a copy, most of them probably stashed under their beds.

That's not to say that *Peyton Place* has been completely lost to time. The book's title is synonymous with secrets and scandal to this very day. But, after selling 60,000 copies in the first ten days of its release and more than 12 million worldwide between then and now, the book had gone out of print for several years. Interest in the story that made Grace Metalious a household name was revived thanks in part to several people. Ardis Cameron, University of Southern Maine's Director of American and New England Studies, deserves much credit for talking Northeastern University Press into reprinting the paperback edition of the book, which happened in 1999. (Ms. Cameron also wrote an excellent biography of the book, 2015's *Unbuttoning America.)* In David Halberstam's Pulitzer Prize-winning book *The 1950s*, which was later turned into a popular seven-part documentary for The History Channel, he also would assert the prominent place *Peyton Place* had when it came to defining the decade. *Peyton Place* was, once again, having a moment.

Grace Metalious is not usually the first author that comes to mind when the topic of New Hampshire authors gets raised. *Peyton Place,* in the minds of many, is linked to Maine and not the Granite State, thanks to Camden being used as the location for much of the movie. This is despite the fact that Grace was born and raised in Manchester, New Hampshire and her novels are almost uniquely New Hampshire books, dealing with small towns in a state known for its small towns. Also lost to literary trivia is that *Peyton Place*, "the book that shocked the nation," is actually based on a very true-life crime that occurred in New Hampshire in the late 1940s. It was a well-known murder in its day. One that made headlines across the country and captivated the nation for many months, just as a decade later the nation would be captivated by *Peyton Place* and outrageous stories about the book's author. Today the only mention you'll hear of the crime, if it's mentioned at all, is usually just a bare line or two linking it to the creation of the novel.

While "ripped from the headlines" might be the buzzword trend today for books and television shows, the phrase was unknown 1950s when *Peyton Place* hit bookstore shelves. *In Cold Blood*, Truman Capote's 1966 novel about the killing of the Kansas-based Clutter family, is often credited as the first true crime novel. But that in no way means that readers had not been interested in the transgressions of others long before Capote and Harper Lee went to Holcomb, Kansas. Pulp-style true crime magazines were wildly popular in the 1940s and 1950s, the very decades when Grace Metalious was growing into a writer. Initially these magazines were filled with fictionalized accounts of crimes from the more distant past. In time they began to turn to oftentimes lurid and sensationalized accounts of current crimes. During their heyday more than two hundred different titles of these small cheaply printed magazines could be found in drug stores and liquor stores across the country. Estimates say that at its peak this genre was selling six million copies every month. The granddaddy of them all was *True Detective,* which boasted a circulation of two million during these golden years. Other popular monthly titles included *True Police*

Cases, *Real Detective Magazine*, *Startling Detective*, and *True Crime Cases*. In general, what they all shared was that they featured almost pin-up style full-color covers: scared-looking women in filmy bras and slips or cigarette smoking redheads were popular. They had tabloid-style slogans that invariably included words like 'confession,' 'sorority girl,' 'passion,' or 'sin'. You would have thought sales would have suffered, as more than one reader must have felt it was false advertising. The sex generally started and stopped at the front cover. Murders were the crime most widely turned into stories for the pages of these editions, with a few kidnappings and cons thrown in for variety, but the sex was only hinted at and the word rape was never, ever used. A number of later lauded authors got their start with this type of writing: Dashiell Hammett and Elmore Leonard's first published pieces graced sensational pulp magazines. The reading public had an interest in true crime tales even if the term, as a genre of its own, was not quite established yet.

Grace Metalious wasn't even the only author of her time to turn a real-life crime into a notorious novel. The year before *Peyton Place* hit bookstore shelves Vladimir Nabokov released *Lolita*, to just as much outcry and scandal. While certainly a better-known book these days to readers, it has always been less well known that *Lolita* is as inspired by the headlines as *Peyton Place*.

The story of *Lolita* had been in the works for years when Nabokov was so fed up with the unfinished manuscript that he tried twice to burn it— stopped only by the quick actions of his wife. It wasn't until Nabokov picked up the newspaper and read of the sad, strange tale of a girl named Sally Horner that he was able to finish his novel that would go on to sell more than sixty-million copies.

Sally Horner was a Camden, New Jersey fifth-grader in 1948 when she succumbed to peer pressure and shoplifted a five-cent notebook from her town's Woolworths. Horner, by all accounts otherwise a good girl, could never have guessed the series of events that would unravel from that small act of larceny. As she left the store with the pilfered notebook, she was stopped by a man named Frank La Salle, who falsely identified himself as an FBI agent. La Salle was not only not a member of law enforcement; he had also recently been released from prison for molesting pre-pubescent girls.

Telling Sally that would turn her in for her crime if she didn't do as he said La Salle convinced the girl to tell her mother that he was the father of a similarly aged school friend. Under the guise of inviting Sally along for a family trip to the Jersey Shore, La Salle, who had no children at all, kidnapped her. La Salle, Sally in tow, traveled across the country from hotel to apartment to hotel, saying Sally was his daughter, while repeatedly raping and abusing the child. It was not until a concerned neighbor in California started to question Sally that the girl finally broke down and admitted what was happening. Twenty-one months after being kidnapped Sally Horner, with the help of her neighbor Ruth Janisch, called the police and her anxious family back in New Jersey.

La Salle initially continued to insist that he was Sally Horner's father. Finally, under the weight of all of the evidence against him, he admitted the truth. Sally was only 11 when she was abducted, she returned home just a few weeks shy of her 13th birthday. La Salle pled guilty to his crimes against her and was sentenced to 35 years in prison under the Mann Act. When asked why he was pleading guilty La Salle said "I am guilty, and I am willing to go in and plead guilty. The sooner the better."[2] Later he added that saving Sally Horner from the publicity and stress of testifying against him was part of his motivation to confess.

Sally Horner, sadly, did not have the happy ending she deserved after her 21 months in captivity. She and her mother stayed in the same town after the trial ended despite the Camden County prosecutor advising Horner's mother that they should move, change their names, and take up new lives. The Horner family, led by a single parent, probably did not have the funds needed to make such a drastic life change.

Instead, Sally continued on much as she had before her abduction. But, of course, nothing was really the same. Her mother never discussed what happened, not with Sally, not with other family members. Sally received no therapy. At school she found herself an outcast. Two years after her return home, at the age of 15, Sally Horner would use a fake I.D. to convince a 20-year-old man that she was of age. She died on August 18, 1952, when her boyfriend's car slammed headfirst into another, killing her instantly. Frank La Salle would die in prison 16 years later, with some sources claiming he sent flowers to Sally's grave every week until he died.

It was this notice of Sally's death that seems to have first caught Nabokov's attention and helped inspire the last half of his book, the same way a small-town murder in northern New Hampshire would be the spark that helped Grace Metalious complete her novel. Besides their true crime roots, *Lolita* and *Peyton Place* share a lasting impact on the cultural zeitgeist. Both books were as scandalous in their time as they are today. However, they are also very different works by very different authors. While both books came to fruition as a direct result of tragic crimes, how Grace Metalious handled the inspiration behind her book is not at all how Nabokov handled his interest in Sally Horner's abduction.

Grace Metalious was always willing to give credit where credit was due. *Peyton Place* was just as much a work in progress when she heard about Barbara and Sylvester Roberts as *Lolita* had been when Nabokov came across the news report on Sally Horner's death. While Grace was always willing to talk about the headline she had ripped, Nabokov and his wife insisted that Sally Horner's story had played no part in *Lolita*. This denial came even though she is mentioned, by name, in the pages of the very novel they denied had anything to do with her. It comes later in the book's pages when Humbert Humbert faces a rare moment of self-doubt and wonders, "Had I done to Dolly, perhaps, what Frank La Salle, a fifty-year-old mechanic, had done to eleven-year-old Sally Horner in 1948?"

During the firestorm of publicity that came after *Lolita* was published in the United States, Nabokov never mentioned Sally Horner. In the 1960s a reporter first drew a connection between the fictitious Delores Haze and the very real Sally Horner but Nabokov, and his ever-vigilant wife, both denied there was any connection. It was not until long after Vladimir Nabokov died that a scholar of his work first really explored how Sally Horner had impacted the novel. Then in 2018 Sarah Weinman, a true-crime writer and journalist, would dig deeper into what the Nabokovs knew and when they knew it, during the creation of the final form of the novel. She published a book that makes a compelling case for Delores as Sally in thin disguise.

This is in sharp contrast to how Grace Metalious handled the true crime aspect of her bestselling page-turner. In 1956, even as reporters swarmed the small town of Gilmanton trying to show it was the "real-life" Peyton Place, few showed any real interest in the murder of Sylvester Roberts. Grace mentioned the crime several times in interviews, almost as a defense for the book that was causing so much ruckus, but it never piqued much interest.

Inspiration from real life is pretty par for the course for novels of any genre. "Write what you know" is the mantra drilled into the head of every writer at the start of learning their craft. It doesn't take anything away from the creative efforts of an author to acknowledge what real-life events might have caught their attention and become a jumping-off point for their own imaginings. Some readers will never care if Delores Haze is Sally Horner, or if Selena Cross is really

Barbara Roberts. Many readers will wonder why it matters at all.

But it does matter. Because tucked inside of these stories we read are real people with real lives. Instead of the books breathing some small sort of life back into those who are no longer here the books, in some ways, have obscured the very real victims that are at the core of them. Though, just as seen in the fictional *Peyton Place*, the question of who the victim is and is not is not always as clear-cut as it was in the case of Sally Horner and Frank La Salle.

In *The Real Lolita* Sarah Weinman writes, "What drove me then and galls me now is that Sally's abduction defined her entire short life. . . After Sally died, her family rarely mentioned her or what had happened. They didn't speak of her in awe, or pity, or scorn. She was only an absence."[3]

In a very similar way the story of Barbara and Sylvester Roberts has been shrouded by the large and looming shadow of the novel that should have shared their story. Inside the pages of *Peyton Place* are people who deserve to have their true stories told.

Chapter One

Childhood is not the best years of your life.
— Grace Metalious, quoted in "The Girl from 'Peyton Place'"

When Grace Metalious told her life story, she always started with a lie. It had been an affectation since high school for Metalious, who was born Marie Grace De Repentigny, to claim that at birth she had been given the rather fanciful and unwieldy name Grace Marie Antionette Jeanne d 'Arc de Repentigny. When she first started telling the silly story, she probably could never have imagined that one day she'd be famous enough for someone to bother to take a peek at her birth certificate and catch her in the lie. In Emily Toth's book on Metalious' life, *Inside Peyton Place*, she calls the extra middle names "the warrior saint and the foolish queen,"4 Grace's first literary creations. But, just like the invented middle names, this is also not quite the truth.

Grace had always been drawn to writing, even at a very young age. As a small child, raised in the sort of household where she would always be sharing a bedroom with her younger sister, Grace would escape to the bathroom at her Aunt Georgie's house. Moving a small flat stool and some paper next to the bathtub Grace created her first writing desk. Locked in this cool porcelain room of her own, Metalious would write poems, unflattering caricatures of her family members, and the first short stories that would, like seeds, later grow into the novels that would make her famous.

Grace Metalious, who would become famous for her portrayals of small towns, was born into a close-knit French-Canadian immigrant family in Manchester, New Hampshire on September 8, 1924. Then, as now, Manchester was the largest city in the Granite State. But this must be put into proper perspective. The entire state of New Hampshire had less than half a million residents the year Metalious was born- easy to see why New Hampshire is known as a state of small towns. Even as the largest city in the state Manchester was not a huge urban jungle. The Manchester of Grace's childhood was still in many ways a company town, just as it had been at its inception when the Amoskeag Manufacturing Company first built the textile mills there. In time the mills complex created by Amoskeag would cover over eight million square feet, the equivalent of the former World Trade Center in New York City. At the height of the company's boom years, the mills employed nearly twenty-thousand Manchester residents, most of whom also lived in Amoskeag owned apartments and spent their paychecks in Amoskeag owned stores. The French-Canadian immigrant community Grace was born into operated like a small town within a larger city.

But Grace's mother held her working-class roots in disdain. Instead of being raised with the support of their community, the family lived in a grey no-man's land. Her mother, Laurette De Repentigny, refused to live in "Petit Canada," as the west side of Manchester was known. Instead, the family lived as close to the posh and exclusive north side of the city as they could afford, in a rented house on the corner of Bridge and Ash Street. Laurette spoke American accented English and refused to work in the mills like the rest of her family. She even splurged and had Grace, who was her first child, in a local hospital instead of at home attended by a midwife as was the custom of the poorer classes at the time. Laurette De Repentigny, as a woman interested in upwards mobility, would have felt that her family, mill workers through and through, were an anchor holding her back. Grace's grandmother, who moved in with the young parents to help raise the baby, spoke only French and it must have rankled Laurette to have her daughter speak the language fluently due to this influence.

This was a time of transition. Not just for the immigrant family, trying to leave behind their traditional roots, but for women across New England. While, in some respects, Manchester was a conservative town life for its residents centered around the Amoskeag Mills more than it did around the church. With women working hand in hand at the textile looms right beside the men it is not surprising that the fight for women's rights touched on this community early. Grace's family, one where the men disappeared early and leave the women behind to run the household and work in the mills to support the family, would have been right at the center of these debates. It was an early lesson for the young writer about just what women were capable of.

Poverty may have driven many women to the hard and dangerous work in the mills, but it was not just the women of the lower classes who were making careers outside the house. The same year as Grace's birth the Manchester Police Commission recommended that female officers be hired—and that they be hired at the same pay as any man on the force. But women weren't just equals in fighting crime. Even while the nearby *Portsmouth Herald* lamented about a crime wave being perpetuated by young men aged 18 to 22 (the *Herald* placed the blame on the home lives of the boys, namely their mothers), women were giving the boys a run for their money for the "Most Wanted" title. In the rough, sometimes seemingly lawless, little city of Manchester women were as involved with committing crimes as they were at keeping the peace. At the same time women were being invited to apply as police officers a young lady, often described as a "bobbed-haired bandit" shocked New England when she held up men in Salisbury, Vermont before going on a cross-state car chase with the local police. That same year Zona Huntoon of Berlin, New Hampshire would be convicted of murder in the second degree for leading a group of four men in the murder of another woman.

Grace, who once rather famously told an interviewer that all she wanted was everything and that she wanted it all the time, grew up in a strange sort of in-between place. This was not just because of her mother's choice of neighborhood but because of the stories Laurette would tell. The family was never rich, never even middle class. As a child Grace was moved to ten different apartments in just about as many years, all as far to the fringes of Little Canada as Laurette could get. As an adult Grace would say that Laurette "thought she was better than anyone else and that her family was better than most."[5] Some would even say that Grace's inclination to exaggeration came from Laurette who, throughout her life, claimed that her father was a French Count. She hunted through flea markets and enjoyed going to auctions to bid on cheap antiques that she later would tell people were family heirlooms brought over directly from France. Laurette would always tell her daughters to marry well, which to her meant not just someone with money but a *gentleman* with money. Grace, growing up in a poor family in increasingly run-down apartments, abandoned by her father, was told she did not have to wash dishes or make her bed because someday she would marry into a different kind of family and would never be expected to do those things for herself.

A sister, Doris, but always known as Bunny to her friends and family, was born two years after Grace. Laurette instructed both girls about the finer things in life—chauffeurs, fancy Parisian restaurants, things she had never seen in her lifetime nor had any real reason to believe they would ever see or experience in their lives either. Laurette also harbored lofty literary ambitions for herself. She dreamed of selling stories to *Harper's Bazaar* but never got an acceptance from the prestigious magazine. In their series of shabby apartments Laurette displayed beautiful leather-bound editions of classic books while making Grace hide her paperback copies of *Nancy Drew* mysteries in the bedroom she shared with Bunny. These things were all cultural stepping-stones for Laurette, who handmade her daughters' clothes but taught them to say they were purchased in the nicer boutiques on Manchester's Elm Street. The finer things in life for Laurette did not just mean nice things that money could buy, it meant culture, theater, and literature.

Whatever airs the De Repentigny family wanted to put on got steadily harder as Grace grew older and the Depression began in earnest. As times got tough her mother was forced to turn to the hated mill work that she had looked down on for so long. But in 1936 the Amoskeag, the largest mill network in the city, closed and even that contemptible career was no longer an option. That same year Laurette officially filed for divorce from Grace's father, who had been absent for some time. The court required that he support the family, ordering him to pay a whopping $10 a week total in child support for both girls. It did little to improve their circumstances.

Perhaps because of her mother's insistence that she would marry well and be a lady of leisure, Grace was an indifferent student. The one academic thing she loved was reading. Like many writers she found refuge in the public library, where she pretended to be bringing books to her mother so she could gain access to the books on the shelves in the adult section of the library. By the fourth grade she was writing as voraciously as she read.

"She spoke truths, though she embellished them."[6] George Metalious, her future husband, said of her after her death. Nowhere was this more seen than in her writing. One of her earliest known works was about an imaginary brother, though like all of Grace's best creations there was a grain of truth hidden inside the lie. Her mother Laurette had born one son, a stillbirth, a couple of years after the births of her girls. Grace's fantasy literary version of her brother adored her. The teacher to whom she handed in this assignment did not love it as much, pointing out that Grace did not have a brother. It was a young writer's first lesson that an almost truth could get her into more trouble than things she made up entirely. But it was not a lesson she learned well.

By seventh grade the imaginary brother stories were gone, replaced by her first known novel, a mystery. Interestingly, Grace never submitted any of her teenage pieces out to publishers or magazines as far as can be told. She wouldn't publish her first short piece until March 1960, which would place it after the release of two best-selling novels, when *Glamour Magazine* would run her short story "Edna Brown and Her Prince Charming." While her mother Laurette may have been driven to be published, Grace was only interested in making life into a little bit more of an interesting story.

Grace's first public creative outlet wouldn't be published stories— it was the theater. In high school she fell in with two boys, the group considered themselves self-proclaimed bohemians. First, they joined the drama club at the local YMCA, but their ideas were too strange for that group and they didn't last long. Together they then put on a play called "Speaking of Angels" in the garage of a neighbor. Grace was both the playwright of "Speaking of Angels" and played its lead role. Their big break would come when a local theater group took up home in the basement of the Unitarian Church that just so happened to be across the street from Manchester's Central High School, where they were all students. Because the theater group had no real funding, they had to write their own plays. It was a role that Grace was singularly built for.

As in some of her previous writing attempts Grace quickly faced censor. The Unitarian minister objected to her production when he discovered the boys would be dressed in drag and playing female roles, a necessity due to the lack of girls interested in acting with the group. The woman who had formed the group, a young wife and Sunday School teacher at the church, went to bat for the kids. The show did indeed go on, but the minister stayed home out of protest. For one weekend, for a mere twenty-five cents, Manchester residents could watch Grace's creation, "Lulubelle Snapgarter," come to life. Played by a male high school senior wearing his mother's shoes and a bra filled with water balloons, Lulubelle Snapgarter danced and sang about the dangers of big city life for close to an hour. Despite the objections of the Unitarian minister the play was a hit and probably gave Grace the first confidence boost she needed as a young writer and a performer.

The theater group only lasted for one year but because of it Grace found her next steppingstone into the creative life. She befriended the organist at the Unitarian church, Bob Athearn, and his wife. The high school girl became a frequent visitor to their home. In reality the Athearn house became more than just a refuge from her increasingly tumultuous relationship with Laurette, it became a true home away from home for the young writer. She and her friends could drop in, drink Jesus Juice (a drink of their own creation, a concoction of gin and grape juice) while they spent hours talking about art and philosophy. The Athearn's home was filled with books. Grace and her friends would read Shakespeare aloud while classical music played on the record player.

Behind the scenes throughout all of Grace's childhood was George Metalious, a former neighbor and friend of Grace's who would, in time, become first her boyfriend and then her husband. This burgeoning relationship was also one of the contributing factors to the increasingly frosty relations between mother and daughter. George had several strikes against him in the eyes of Grace's family. First, he was Greek. Second, he was not at all the kind of wealthy gentleman Laurette felt either of her daughters deserved.

Laurette, as to be expected, cautioned Grace against dating him. But in a private letter Grace called George the first person in her life who made her feel special. The young couple wanted to get married right out of high school but both families objected strenuously.

Grace and George compounded the scandal of dating "outside their own" by deciding to live together in sin since their families wouldn't approve of the marriage. This was in 1943 when co-habitation was just not done, not in big urban cities and definitely not in small-town New Hampshire. The young couple struggled to find a landlord that would even rent to them. Eventually persistence paid off. But just as Grace and George found a landlord who was happy to take their monthly rent check without them sharing the same last name, the families relented. On February 27, 1943, their wedding was held.

It was almost a given that most of the attendees thought Grace was pregnant. They couldn't imagine either family allowing their child to marry the other. At the time the French and Greek families in Manchester did not mix in that way. On top of this, Grace was only 18 years old; George a full two months shy of his 18th birthday. In later years Grace would tell reporters that nine months after the nuptials she threw a big party to show off her flat stomach to all of their friends and family. But, like many of Grace's most frequently told anecdotes, this too was something both more and less than the truth. Nine months after the wedding Grace may have had a flat stomach— but she also held a newborn baby in her arms. It was seven months after her wedding day that she gave birth to her first child, a daughter they named Marsha.

In 1959 Grace would write that, "George eventually came to the conclusion that I hadn't an honest bone in my body, he was absolutely right."[7] But, like any good raconteur, Grace didn't consider these fabrications lies, merely amusing stories. George didn't see them in the same light. Grace's young age, and an upbringing that stressed she would never need to work, did not prime her to meet the rigors of the clean and orderly domesticated life that was expected at the time. Among Grace's little white lies was her ability to cook. While George was out working, Grace would bring a bag of groceries to her grandmother's apartment. Grand'Mere would turn the bags of ingredients into a fine meal and hand it back to Grace. As long as she brought the cooked dinner home before George returned from work, she could claim the meal was her own creation. The arrangement worked out fine for everyone involved, at least until sister Bunny let the truth slip to George.

Grace was further able to stretch the truth about her domestic abilities because George, who had tried to enlist and was turned down for his poor eyesight, was then drafted within days of turning 18. While he went off to bootcamp, Grace returned to her mother's latest apartment and, just as she had for years, shared a bedroom with her sister Bunny. Even though she was back in the family home for the majority of her pregnancy, the birth of Marsha was suffered alone. Having family in the delivery room is a more modern invention. It was a traumatic experience but one that Grace was happy to have done while George was stationed elsewhere. When the doctors told Grace she should never attempt to have another child, she was able to simply hide that advice from her family and her enlisted husband.

Five weeks after the difficult birth, Grace packed up her newborn daughter and took off for Texas, where George was stationed. She was tired of living with her mother and sister after going to all the trouble of getting married just to escape them. Perhaps knowing that George would try to talk her out of the move, Grace kept the trip quiet until just before her arrival at Fort Barkley. In St. Louis Grace stopped off to send a telegram to her husband. It read simply: "Will be in Abilene tomorrow with our new family addition." With so little forewarning that his wife and child were on their way, George had no time to switch guard duty to meet them and no time to arrange housing. It was an army buddy of George's that would meet Grace and Marsha in Abilene, not her husband.

Following George throughout his military career was not at all what Grace had hoped for when she left New Hampshire. In a replay of her own childhood, she, and Marsha, bounced from one shoddy living space to another but this time, instead of each new home being in more or less the same neighborhood in the same small city they had to uproot and go from state to state, often with little notice. A two-room shack in Texas, located near Camp Barkley, was replaced by a single room with a hot plate in Springfield, Missouri when George was transferred. George wanted his young family back in New Hampshire where Grace could get help from their families with the baby. However prudent that might have been, Grace saw it as nothing but rejection.

Grace and Marsha eventually did succumb to the realities of the situation and returned to Manchester, New Hampshire. Grace moved in with her Grand'Mere, who had a five-bedroom apartment she was struggling to pay for. For the first time in her life Grace would get a job—falling into the same pattern her own mother had before her, with her Grandmother raising her baby while she worked a string of menial jobs. Still, it was not all work and no play for Grace Metalious. Under the guise of chaperoning her sister Bunny, Grace had a full social schedule. Once, when George returned home on leave for a quick visit, he would find Grace just getting back from her date with a man in the Air Force. Grace admitted she had been dating— but she swore up and down to George that none of the relationships had turned sexual.

When George returned home for good from the war, he expected to find a bank account full to the brim with a down payment on the young couple's first home. Instead, he found that Grace was three weeks behind on her rent and had been supporting her Grand'Mere, her Aunt Georgie, her mother, and sister Bunny. The couple had little time to replenish their nest egg as Grace fell pregnant just a few months after George got home and Grace became too sick to work. Soon after, now saddled with two small children and a host of poorly paying jobs, Grace and George moved into a tenement in Manchester that had been put aside for veterans and their families. It was not at all the cultured and privileged life Laurette had promised her, though there is little indication that Grace had ever believed that was something the future had in store for her anyway.

George, on the other hand, was desperate to get out of the cycle of poverty. Looking for a better life for his ever-growing family George decided to go to the University of New Hampshire on the G.I. Bill and get a degree. Having George in school and not working full-time was a crushing hardship for the young family but it was the only thing that could ensure their long-term survival. On the seacoast George lived on campus while Grace lived separately in a furnished room that did not allow children. The two Metalious children, Marsha and Christopher (called Mike by the family) were just one and five years old and lived with relatives during the week. The only time they were all able to be together as a family under one roof was on the weekends, and that was only if they were willing to stay with George's mother.

The family was able to all be together again in a more permanent way when George found them an apartment in nearby Portsmouth, in a building filled with other students. With her interest in literature, it should have been an ideal environment for Grace. But she was always keenly aware that she had no higher education herself and that she was only there as George's wife. At the Portsmouth apartment, as when they were first married in Manchester, Grace did not fit the mold expected of a 1950s housewife— and suffered for it. Neighbors in the student-filled building commented, often openly, on what they saw as her lack of interest in her children or how messily she kept their home. The children especially were a sticking point for the neighbors, who would find them outside their door with no mother in sight. What these neighbors didn't know was that Grace was hard at work inside the slovenly apartment. With no room of her own, she was writing.

Chapter Two

"Often Lisa thought bitterly of the ideas she had held on "college life" before coming to Denton, ideas and images culled from a hundred magazine stories and as many movies. Where were the convertibles, the secret bottles of liquor, the gay young men and their wild girl friends?"
— Grace Metalious, "The Tight White Collar"

"I am trapped in a cage of poverty and mediocrity," Grace would write later about George's college years at U.N.H. "If I don't get out, I'll die."8 The birth of a third child, a little girl they named Cynthia, had profound effects on Grace's life and her views of herself as a woman. As with her previous pregnancies, she was told she should have no more children, that to do so would cost the lives of both mother and child. This time the warning came across as much more dire and Grace, living in a time before birth control pills were widely available, got a tubal litigation to ensure there would be no more Metalious children. Instead, resentment grew in her belly. Grace was tired of shopping for the groceries, raising three small children, and working long hours to pay a seemingly insurmountable pile of bills while George got to have the full college experience.

While neighbors, and later book critics, would make much of "the type of mother" she must be to keep such a dirty house and write such a dirty book the feminine ideals of the time were still hard at work on Grace. Later in life when her publisher asked her to write a short author's bio, at a time when she was the famous author of an even more infamous book, Grace would write only "I was born. I married. I reproduced." It was less a biography than it was an affirmation that she had, in her own small way, fulfilled what she saw as her job as a woman. But, while Grace struggled with what she saw as her failure as a woman, there was a certain relief as well. With no more pregnancies looming, there was time for Grace to fill her life with something more.

Grace knew the only escape from the two biggest issues in her life, poverty and mediocrity, was her writing. What exactly she was writing at this time is not entirely clear. She was known for making up charming stories for the kids that ran around the apartment development, but any works she made for a less juvenile audience were kept closer to the vest. Perhaps because of her insecurities about her absence of an education or because of her lack of connection to her neighbors, she never talked much about what she was creating during the years George was in school. Some of the Portsmouth neighbors would say they saw pieces of themselves in *Peyton Place* when it was published years later. And we know from when Grace was a child that she tended to write about the people around her. George Metalious, in his tell-all book published the year after Grace's death, said during this time she created some short stories about Norman Page and Hester Goodale. These characters would one day become secondary characters in *Peyton Place*. George Metalious also said that the first early drafts of the book that would become *The Tight White Collar* were created at this time, in a slightly different form.

We do know of two or three short stories she wrote during this time. They show just how much the real world that surrounded her inspired her literary creations. One short story was set in an old mill town, much like the Manchester of her youth. We see a fictionalized mention of the 1950 suicide of a beloved local Durham music teacher, rumored to have come about because of his struggles with his sexual affiliation. This would pop up again in the later novel *The Tight White Collar*. Grace's theater friends from high school were gay, it is probably one of the reasons why the story, spread quickly around the U.N.H. rumor mill resonated with her. Some of her surviving short stories are set in college towns that more or less mimic Durham where the University of New Hampshire remains located to this day. None of these stories would be submitted for publication at the time of their writing even though there were thriving markets for short works in the magazines that flourished during this time. Grace, in her mind, still could not make the jump from writing to being a *published* writer.

Grace did make a different kind of big leap at this time though, going from a student's wife to being the wife of a teacher when George graduated and began a job up north at the high school in Belmont, New Hampshire. Grace did not find the role of a teacher's wife to be a happy one. She was expected to attend school functions and to chaperone the cheer leaders when the school's basketball team had an away game. She felt she had to be charming and to wear a proper skirt and blouse instead of the jeans and plaid men's shirts she wore as her everyday uniform. Grace would say the result was that she "ran to my work more and more. I tried to escape from reality by writing oceans of words."[9]

Grace did make a few friends in the Lakes Region in northern New Hampshire even though the neighbors there took as poor of a view of her housekeeping as her neighbors in Durham had. Jeanne Gallant, whose horse farm was next to the house Grace would buy after publishing *Peyton Place*, shared the story of a neighbor who was friendly enough with the burgeoning writer that he lent her a car so she could go get groceries for her family. A few days passed, with no Grace, no car, and no idea where either had ended up. The neighbor felt he had no choice but to report the car stolen at the police station. The Police Chief was as aware as the rest of the small town that Grace had a reputation for being unreliable. He was not at all concerned about the missing car. The Police Chief said that he was sure Grace was around somewhere and would return the car eventually.

Grace was indeed somewhere. After buying enough groceries to last George and the kids for a few days, she had taken off for New York City so she could start knocking on agent's doors. Yes, after years of writing with no interest in publication 1953 marked Grace's first submission— a compilation of short stories from her U.N.H. years that she sent to a big New York publisher. A month later when she had no reply, she took the neighbor's car to go visit publishers and agents in person. The trip overall was a dud. All Grace succeeded in learning was that the publisher wasn't at all interested in her book and that the agents were unimpressed with her short stories and her absence of published works. The anthology would never be published. And the neighbor never lent Grace Metalious a car again.

Word of what Grace was up to got out quickly. Belmont, after all, had only 700 residents so it was impossible to keep any kind of secret especially with Grace's publishing excursion resulting in stolen car reports. Neighbors said she was writing about them. Others said she was already negotiating with a publisher. Eventually, this talk reached the right set of ears: those of a local journalist for *The Laconia Evening Citizen.* Intrigued by the rumors she was hearing this journalist decided to go track down the truth, and the woman, who was behind them. Laurose Wilkens was about to meet Grace Metalious.

Chapter Three

You begin to look for a substitute. Somehow you are going to create something. And then one day you look at your typewriter.
— Grace Metalious

Grace had never been interviewed by a reporter before. For the first time ever, she was getting attention— the good kind of attention— for her writing. That may be why she decided to share her manuscript in progress with Laurose Wilkens. In the journalist, who almost always went by Laurie and not Laurose, she quickly found a kindred spirit even if the two women could not have come from more dissimilar backgrounds.

Laurie Wilkens, nearly a dozen years older than Grace, had grown up in New York City, with summer trips to Europe and a houseful of servants. It was the kind of life that Grace's mother Laurette had always aspired to. Laurie, on the other hand, had completely rejected that lifestyle. She married for love and, after honeymooning in New Hampshire's White Mountains, ended up buying a 200-year-old farmhouse in the tiny town of Gilmanton. When the town was settled in 1727 the story goes that twenty-five of the original residents were members of the Gilman family. In typical Yankee economy Gilmantown quickly became called Gilmanton. Spread across sixty square miles and located just far enough away from Lake Winnipesaukee and Lake Winnisquam to not be bothered by the tourist trade, it had been a small rural community for all of its history. Laurie Wilkins went in search of the solitude; Grace had gone only because of the necessities of her husband's job. But the two women loved books, and music, and theater. It probably helped that both were considered outsiders to those who had grown up in the area. Being from "away" was as much a detriment to the two women's ability to make other women friends as was their interest in un-womanly pursuits like writing and theater.

When the Metalious' Belmont landlord evicted the family because he was worried about the rumors he had heard and could not stand the sound of Grace click-clacking on her old Remington typewriter all day and night it was Laurie Wilkens who swooped in and saved the day. She found a small house, really no more than a shack, and convinced the landlord to accept the family that was quickly gaining a reputation for being a little bit off as tenants. For the sum of $35 a month the ramshackle house, complete with the sign out front naming it "It'll Do," fit their budget.

What it did not fit was the idea that people in the area had about what a house should be. And Grace certainly did not fit their idea of what a 1950s housewife should be. The house was a little gingerbread cottage tucked away on a dirt road, surrounded by flowers and birdhouses. It was a little oddly built, as the owner had taken in foster children for years and tacked on new additions with each new child she took in. But whatever charms "It'll Do" might have had was quickly lost under a layer of clutter and grime. A neighbor would later recall that "It'll Do" was nothing more than "a little shanty house, with dirty dishes everywhere. Everything was covered with grime and dirt except one spotless corner, where Grace kept her typewriter."[10] Grace wasn't interested in cleaning, after all she had a book to write.

Grace also had Laurie not too far from home. Laurie was not just Grace's best friend and a trusted confidant; her big comfortable farmhouse was a home away from home.

Maybe even more a home than "It'll Do" was as Grace seemed to look at that house simply as the place where she would do the challenging work of getting the words down on the page. The real living, the parts that really mattered, happened at the Wilken's farmhouse. Ensconced in the farmhouse's cozy kitchen Laurie would read aloud the pages Grace had worked on that day. The women would laugh and gossip, talking about their favorite books and sharing a bottle of wine.

"There was always excitement about her," Laurie would later tell a biographer. "Everything was a lark."[11]

Even though Laurie was from "away," far away even, she loved this little corner of New Hampshire like a New England native at heart. Her job at the newspaper gave her a wealth of information about Gilmanton and the surrounding towns. And in Grace she found someone who was just as interested in those anecdotes as she was.

Laurose Wilkens died in 2007, but her son John still remembers the family's time with Grace well. He talked about the fondness his mother had for the author, saying that she "and Grace would sit in the evenings and sip beer and mom told her the stories of the town. Thus, *Peyton Place* was born."[12]

One of the stories Laurie Wilkens told Grace about dated back to her first years in New Hampshire. Laurie had just started farming "Shaky Acres," as she dubbed her farm situated about two miles southeast of Gilmanton Corners in what was considered the right part of town. Despite its rural atmosphere New Hampshire has never been known for having very farmable land. What it does have, besides timber and beautiful places to hike and ski, is vast stretches of land that are great for grazing livestock. A Shaky Acres neighbor, seeing Laurie struggle with the agricultural life during her first year on the farm, suggested she try her hand at raising sheep.

At the advice of this same neighbor Laurie made the trip six miles down the road to Gilmanton Iron Works. As in many thinly populated states, the northern reach of New Hampshire has a number of unincorporated townships. Gilmanton Iron Works is one of them. Located near the eastern border of Gilmanton, Gilmanton Iron Works began life as Averytown. At that time, it was the site of a small mining operation, but the venture never quite made enough money to be truly profitable. Even though the mine quickly folded this part of Gilmanton became known as Gilmanton Iron Works, a name it keeps even to this day. While the unincorporated township sits within the borders of Gilmanton, the Iron Works is enough of its own community that it has its own separate zip code, post office, and library. At one point, despite the failure of the iron works, this small town within a town had an entire Main Street style set up of its own, with stores and homes. In 1915 a fire would destroy this ad hoc downtown, taking the Iron Work's church and at least half a dozen homes with it. People continued to live in Gilmanton Iron Works, in fact they still do, but it has never been built up to quite the degree it had been before the fire. The center of Gilmanton Iron Works, in the 1940s as today, consists mostly of a general store and small fire department.

In modern times, there is not much difference between Gilmanton, Gilmanton Iron Works, and Gilmanton Corners, which is the third unincorporated community within the town's borders. All feature small well-kept homes, many with signs outside advertising fresh eggs for sale or snow-plowing services. There are no signs denoting where one of the towns ends and another begins, but it's a distinction locals are still very aware of even if though those from away cannot tell the difference. This was not the case in the 1940s when Laurie Wilkins moved to the area. Looking to buy a few sheep for her farm Laurie found that the meager six miles actually made a world of difference between Gilmanton and Gilmanton Iron Works. Following the directions given to her by her neighbor she found the homestead she was looking for, a solid if weathered, home. It was of the style that real estate agents, optimistically, might refer to as a New Englander. It featured one carefully built traditional colonial house with two large chimneys at the center, and then a jumble of rooms and additions growing out behind it, tacked on higgly-piggly as more space was needed over time. In the distance, half-hidden by the house, Laurie could see what looked like a small, old-fashioned barn with an attached sheep pen.

The place seemed deserted, but a young woman answered the door quickly in response to Laurie's cautious knock. Laurie took a literal step back when the door opened; the girl was an unexpected beauty with long dark hair and deep brown eyes. The young woman wore a stylish purple dress, something that Laurie wouldn't have looked at twice at in New York City but that here, in a tumbledown farmhouse in rural New Hampshire, was as unexpected as dirty overalls would have been in the big city.

When the girl heard why Laurie was there, she insisted that she had no sheep, pen out back notwithstanding. She said they had all been sold off and she didn't know why anyone would have sent Laurie there. Laurie felt rushed out the door. But it was also a feeling she welcomed because, as she would tell Grace Metalious years later, the girl gave her a creepy feeling. It wasn't the dress or the young lady's insistence that the farm had no sheep. No, it was that but also more than that, something to do with the anxious, high-strung energy that came off the girl in waves at finding a neighbor knocking on her door for a perfectly innocuous reason.

Laurie didn't know it at the time, but she had just had a very small brush with infamy. A short time later she would be surprised to see a picture of the girl on the front page of the very paper she wrote for. That September the girl, Barbara Roberts, would confess to a heinous murder. It was a crime that the locals would come to know as “The Sheep Pen Murder,” and it would live on in a much different way within the pages of a fiction novel being written by Grace Metalious years later.

Chapter Four

I just write the truth as I see it. There are no two ways about the truth. It's either truth or it's a lie.
— Grace Metalious, quoted in "The Girl from 'Peyton Place'"

A steady stream of profanities, each one growing louder and more vulgar than the one before it, alerted Barbara Roberts that her father Sylvester, a Merchant Marine, was home. Barbara was a pretty girl, a nice girl, the kind of girl that the people of Gilmanton Iron Works were proud to call one of their own. She had been raising her brother Billy as if he were her own child from the time she was eleven years old when her mother died in 1937. Still mostly a child herself Barbara Roberts had run the household the way a grown woman would, raising her younger brother, keeping house for her father and older brothers when they were home, and helping out on the family farm however she could.

Sylvester Roberts had bought the farm in 1927. He was born in Birmingham, England around 1895, to a long line of sailors and shipbuilders. Sylvester had moved to the United States in the 1920s for the same reason so many young men immigrated at that time— namely to take up work in the many mills and factories that had begun to flourish in the northeast. So many immigrants, from England, Canada, Ireland, and other European countries, flooded the American labor market that they became known as the Great Wave.

Some would say that too many had come. As more and more young men like Sylvester Roberts found their way to American shores the government looked for ways to stem the rising tide of cheap, mostly unskilled, labor. In 1917, capitalizing on the unease created by World War I, the country would enact what is seen as the first widely restrictive immigration laws. Arriving immigrants over the age of 16 were required to prove they could read and write before they were allowed to enter legally. Finding that this did not slow down foreign interest in moving to America The Johnson-Reed Act was put into place in 1924, limiting the number of people that could enter, based on their country of birth. Anyone born in an Asian country other than Japan was barred completely. Sylvester was able to read and write proficiently and was one of those lucky enough to enter the country before the Immigration Act took full effect.

The factory and mill work Sylvester found in the United States was not all that different than he would have found back home in England. Birmingham was, and in some ways still is, a major manufacturing city. But Birmingham was crowded, already heavily polluted, and was not at all the right place for a young man who had dreams of seeing the world and crafting a life that was a little better than what he had grown up with. Sylvester arrived in Boston with his bride, Margery Almedia (formerly Porter). They quickly had three children. Charles Sylvester Roberts was born in 1922, Robert Llewelyn Morris Roberts entered the world in 1923, and Marjory Ava Roberts joined the growing family in 1924. Finding it increasingly difficult to provide for his family in Boston Sylvester moved them all to New York City where he believed there would be better wages.

But living in a small, rented apartment in a tenement building in Brooklyn with three children under the age of five was no better of a life than what the Roberts family had faced in Boston. Before the Immigration Act of 1924 as many as a million people a year passed through New

York City. Even after the restrictions were put in place that number slowed but never stopped entirely. In New York Sylvester Roberts faced more competition, increasingly lower wages, and overcrowded living conditions that would have made Birmingham look like a rural oasis. After the birth of Barbara Roberts on January 27, 1927 the family knew they had to make a change.

Sylvester's two older brothers had also transplanted themselves to American shores, all within a few years of each other. But the other Roberts brothers had chosen an entirely different kind of path, feeling there were more opportunities to be found in America than more of the same factory work they could have done in England. The workers who had flocked to mill work in the cities since the advent of the Industrial Revolution were not just recent immigrants. Many farmers throughout the northeast had found they could no longer compete with the enormous farms of the mid-west and were pushed out of the agricultural life. Many of the household tasks women on the farm used to be responsible for, things like making soap or spinning yarn, were no longer in as much demand since factories were able to mass-produce those things at increasingly affordable prices. As New Englanders quite literally left the family farm behind for the big cities it created an opportunity for others to have their pick of farmland at rock bottom prices. Earnest Roberts was one of these people who went against the trend and eschewed mill work when he immigrated to the United States. He chose a farmer's life and bought a good-sized spread of land in Gilmanton, New Hampshire.

In short order Earnest had become a prosperous poultry farmer. Charles, a third Roberts brother who had achieved some fame in England as a "boy orator" and lecturer for the British Labour Party, had also moved to New Hampshire's Lakes Region. He did even better for himself than Earnest had. Charles, for whom Sylvester would name his first-born son, bought the famed Cogswell Estate in the town of Belmont. This historic farmhouse, built in the early 1700s, predated the town of Belmont and was once home to Governor William Badger, an important politician and mill owner who has been credited with bringing the Industrial Revolution to New Hampshire. Charles had continued lecturing after moving to Belmont, speaking at Rotary Clubs and libraries on a number of different topics, and was well known in the area. He was called "Uncle Charley," not just by his nieces and nephews but by everyone in the region. Seeing how well his brothers had done created a natural incentive for Sylvester to move his family to the Granite State to try and do the same.

Sylvester, probably with some help from his brothers, was able to buy a small farmstead just up the road from his brother Earnest. He raised sheep with the expectation that he would supply wool to the small mills that dotted the north country and the larger ones further south in Manchester and in Lowell, Massachusetts. A fifth and final child, William, was born at that Gilmanton Iron Works farmhouse in 1931. But Sylvester had a restlessness to him even then. He was a small slight man, known for his oversized ten-gallon hat, he spent more time sitting on the post office steps and chatting with neighbors than he did on the farm. Probably because of this the farm, located just off the state route known locally as the Alton-Belmont Road, never quite flourished in the way that the endeavors of the other Roberts brothers did. This was despite the fact that Sylvester had a built-in labor force in the form of his own five children, who were all expected to help out around the farm and do as much of the work as much as any paid, full-grown man would have been.

And help was needed! The hardscrabble farm was tucked into dense woods, two hundred feet off the dirt road, and more than a mile away from its nearest neighbor. Not much grew there and what did, did not sprout up easily. Cows provided just enough milk for the family to consume themselves; the sheep brought in some small amounts of cash but nothing like what Sylvester had hoped for when he moved his family up north. And, like a current running underneath it all, was the deep-seated feeling that this stony plot of land was not where Sylvester Roberts was meant to be.

Then, on April 15, 1938, the family faced a devastating blow. Marjory, Sylvester's wife and mother to all five children, died at the age of 40. Mother Marjory knew that Charles and Robert, aged 16 and 15, were nearly grown and would leave the farm soon as well as she knew that her namesake daughter would be married herself in short time. On her deathbed Marjorie turned to her youngest daughter Barbara, only 11 but already known for her work ethic and steady disposition, and begged her to watch out for Billy, the youngest of the clan, when she was gone. Barbara promised.

The family struggled along for a few more years but with the passing of Mother Marjory it seemed like the heart had gone out of everything. In 1942 Sylvester and his two oldest sons dutifully filled out their draft registrations and then promptly joined the Merchant Marines. Merchant Marines, despite the name, are not members of the military. The civilian members of the Merchant Marines transport cargo and passengers for the military, usually on ships owned by the Federal government, but do not face combat firsthand. Joining up was seen as both a way to support the war effort and to possibly keep from being sent to the front lines if drafted.

As an extra bonus the Roberts men would be off the farm and have the chance to see the wider world outside of New England. The Robertses had, in the way of their ancestors, gone back to the sea again. This left Marjorie, Barbara, and Billy home alone on the Gilmanton Iron Works farm. Eventually, in October of 1945, Marjorie married a boy named Paul from nearby Alton, New Hampshire. She ceased to be Marjorie Roberts and become Marjorie Richards.

With the men of the family away at sea, seeing the world as Merchant Marines and her sister starting her own family, Barbara stayed home. She left school in the ninth grade to keep the farm going and to fulfill the role of mother to her younger brother Billy. Barbara Roberts spent the spring months cutting hay. In the summer she picked whatever berries grew on the edges of the woods surrounding the farm. And she put aside wood through the autumn months to feed into the Roberts Farms two big fireplaces all winter long. With the help of Billy, Barbara slaughtered sheep for fresh meat as was needed.

It was a hard life, but it was the only one she had ever known. And it was not all that different from the lives of other Gilmanton Iron Works residents, even though most of the farms had a grown man to do the hardest parts of the jobs that needed doing. Gilmanton, located in the first foothills of the White Mountains, is only eighteen miles from the state's capital in Concord. But the distance between the rural farming community and the gold-capped state house seemed further in every other way that mattered. It may not have been geographically distant, but it was many miles away when measured by the mind.

It had been a relief to Sylvester to be able to walk away from the responsibilities that came with being tied to the land and the demands of being a single parent. Barbara and Billy were able to do everything that needed to be done on the homestead, their catch as catch can existence supplemented by whatever part of their paychecks Sylvester and their older brothers sent home.

When the pair struggled to make ends meet Barbara got a job as a clerk at Nockle's, the small general store in the center of town. At Nockle's she was popular, both with her fellow employees and with the many town residents who came to do their grocery shopping. Barbara had a reputation for being unfailingly polite but always all business when at the job.

"Everybody liked her," Florence Bordeau, who was a manager at the store during the time Barbara worked there, would say later. "Most young girls don't get along with the older folks, but Barbara was perfect."[13]

Barbara's co-workers marveled at her strength. They called the pretty girl rugged and said she must have been used to heavy lifting. Her farm-hardened muscles made her able to heft giant quarters of beef with no effort when at the store. People said of her, approvingly, that she could do a man's job despite her young age and her gender.

Chapter Five

"She saw hopelessness as an old enemy, as persistent and inevitable as death."
— Grace Metalious, 'Peyton Place'

During these years Sylvester Roberts spent as little time as possible at home. When he wasn't aboard some freighter sailing the seas, he hung around the New York City Mariner's Union Hall, joking with the other mariners. Sylvester Roberts was known as an outgoing and garrulous man. He liked to gamble his paycheck away on card games while waiting for the next ship to come by in need of a crew. Still, every so often, he would send a telegram and let his family know that he was on his way home to New Hampshire for a short visit. The visits were never scheduled; they happened with no regularity. Just every so often the urge to go home would hit Sylvester Roberts and he'd give his children a day or two's worth of notice that he was on his way.

His 1946 holiday visit started off no different than any of those that had come before it. A couple of days before the Christmas holiday Barbara was finishing up her regular shift at Nockle's General Store when she got word that a telegram was waiting for her. She used the store's phone to call the telegram office in nearby Laconia but got no answer. Even so, she was already sure she knew exactly what the message waiting for her would say. It was news she dreaded at any time but now it was coming at the worst possible moment.

Sylvester Roberts had always told his youngest daughter that if she ever neglected to pick him up at the train station when he came home that he would kill her. And here he was, letting them know he was coming home right when the family car wouldn't start and was at the mechanics in Alton. There was a bus, sometimes, that ran intermittently between the train station and a nearby town. But even that option would mean her father, expecting a ride home after taking the train up from New York City, would be walking seven or eight miles through the north country forests. Without the bus that trip became twenty-eight miles, all on foot, across cold country roads during the darkest part of the year.

There was no chance the telegram could be anything other than unwelcome news from Sylvester. He never wrote real letters the way her brothers did, and he only ever sent a telegram when he was on his way home. No one else ever sent telegrams to the Roberts siblings. Barbara was in a panic, knowing that Sylvester, abusive even in the best of times, would be coming home enraged. Her fear was great enough that, knowing her father could call at any moment asking for a ride from the train station, Barbara tried to track down Frank Dowst.

Frank Dowst, in the way of exceedingly small towns, was both the school janitor and the town's Police Chief. Just a few months before Barbara had started to confide in him about the conditions at home, which she described as intolerable. This had happened the past October, which was the last time her father had come to visit. The Police Chief had walked into Nockle's for a loaf of bread on his way home from work and found Barbara crying into her apron. The girl was alone, all the other Nockle's employees had left for dinner, and at first, she tried to explain away her tears as the result of stomach pains. Dowst, having known Barbara for most of her life knew she was not the kind of girl given over to emotion, and he gently began to question her as to what was really wrong. Eventually she could hold the truth in no longer. With a deep sob she told Dowst that terrible violent fights occurred every time her father came home on furlough. She was scared for herself and also scared for the well-being of the younger brother that was more like a son to her.

"You have no idea of the kind of life I lead when my father is home,"[14] the young lady had told him, words that would haunt a year later when the full truth of conditions at the Roberts farm became known to everyone.

That fall Barbara had told Dowst things were bad. But she had not elaborated on just how terrible things really were. Dowst had not been overly concerned with what she said, most teenagers, even ones as level-headed and hard-working as Barbara Roberts, complained about their parents from time to time. Barbara had told him that Sylvester sometimes threatened to shoot her and Billy but that seemed like a gross exaggeration to the Police Chief. He did not know Sylvester well, no one in town really did with how often he was out to sea, but the man was known for his humor and goodwill. The people of Gilmanton Iron Works had loved Barbara's mother and Sylvester had long been something of a fixture in town. On his short jaunts back to New Hampshire to visit his family he would spend his afternoons back on the steps of the post office, just as he had before he left. From his perch on the cement stairs, he'd keep up the same kind of jovial good cheer as he did in the New York City Mariner's Union Hall. Sitting on the post office steps he entertained patrons with his wild tales of adventure on the high seas, talking about places most of them would never visit themselves. Dowst had heard Sylvester had a temper, a few people in town had mentioned so here and there over the years, but he had never seen any evidence of it himself so he never paid much mind to those infrequent mutterings.

Even more important than what people thought of Sylvester was what they thought of the whole family. In the Lakes Region of New Hampshire, the Roberts family was well thought of by their neighbors. Surely the brother of a lauded speaker and a wealthy farmer could not be so cruel to his own children. Dowst had told Barbara to leave the farm if she didn't like it, the girl was, after all, of age now. But Barbara had refused. Billy would be on his own if she left, not only having to keep the farm going by himself, he'd also be the sole recipient of her father's rages on the odd occasions that he came home. Barbara's greatest fear was that Sylvester, finding her gone, would shoot her brother Billy in his rage at her actions.

Now, three months after the conversation with Dowst, Barbara was at her wits end thinking of what would happen when the call came from the train station and she could not give her father the ride home that he expected and demanded. She had thought she'd have more time after her father's last visit to the farm. Remembering how kind Dowst had been, even if he had not seemed to realize the severity of her situation, Barbara decided she was ready to confess all. She bundled up against the December chill, pulling her warm winter coat over her Nockle's work apron, and walked through the center of Gilmanton Iron Works and into Gilmanton proper looking for Dowst. The increasingly distressed girl had no idea that Frank Dowst was out of town for the holiday and could be of no help to her. Unable to think of a way out of her situation Barbara returned to the Roberts' farm to wait for her father's phone call.

When the dreaded phone call came Barbara was home, but she didn't have the guts to answer it. She knew there was nothing she could say that would calm her father's anger; no excuse would be good enough, no reason reasonable enough for him to accept that none of this was her fault and that she, as always, was doing the best she could. Instead, she hid in the pantry and did what she did best— she went to work. Tucked away in the pantry with a warm iron and a pile of freshly laundered clothes she put her head down and ignored the phone. The warm iron made the pantry feel cozy and safe, but she knew it was an illusion just waiting to be shattered. Eventually Sylvester would walk through the front door and Barbara would have hell to pay.

Barbara sent her brother Billy off to do some last-minute Christmas shopping, accompanied by their older sister Marjorie. When she heard the cussing of her irate father coming up the driveway, she took note of the time: it was just turning a quarter past 6:00 pm. This was notable because it was much earlier than it should have been. Her father must have been able to hitch a ride home when he realized his second youngest child would not be coming to get him. Some men would have taken the gift of the ride as a small concession and let it act as a balm to their anger. But Sylvester Roberts was not one of those men. He was as steaming mad as he would have been if he had walked the entire twenty-eight miles in the December cold by foot, one chilly footstep after the next.

What happened next would remain a secret until almost a year later. Besides his daughter Barbara, whoever had picked up Sylvester Roberts and given him a ride home that night would be the last person to see the Merchant Marine alive.

Chapter Six

I used to try very hard not to cry because I had a reputation for never crying. I maintained that tears were the weapon of the weak and that I had no use for women who used them.

— Grace Metalious, quoted in "The Girl from 'Peyton Place"

It was Charles, a Lieutenant commander in the Merchant Marines and the oldest of the Roberts siblings, who first raised the alarm about Sylvester having gone missing. He and Robert Roberts, the second born of the clan and now a Petty Officer, came home in April of 1947 for a family visit and asked about their father's whereabouts. They had not seen him in some time. Barbara said Sylvester was out at sea and had not been home for many months. The two older brothers asked about his Christmas time visit but Barbara demurred. She and Billy had celebrated alone, she told them, adding that Sylvester had not telegraphed or shown up that year.

No, she assured Charles, he hadn't called from the train station and she had not heard from him since. It seemed a little odd to Charles, but he knew as well as anyone else how much his father preferred being out to sea than stuck on the family farm with the children he had left behind to raise themselves. The people of Gilmanton Iron Works also accepted the explanation easily enough on the rare occasions that Sylvester's whereabouts came up. It did not surprise any of them that Sylvester was away from home for an extended period of time.

That summer the Humane Society alerted Frank Dowst that they had received a complaint about animals being neglected on the Roberts Farm. Dowst went to see what was going on, it seemed out of character for Barbara to ignore the animals, but he found no one home. In the barn some cows and horses were milling around out of their stalls, but they had plenty of food and water. Unlike other times he had been to the farm there were no sheep. Dowst didn't notice anything unusual in the barn or sheep pen. He did notice a pane of glass had been broken in the kitchen door, but he didn't think much of it. Later that day he would report back to the Humane Society that everything was just fine on the farm.

But Barbara was not fine. That August, rather abruptly, she packed only a few articles of clothing and left the Roberts farm for good. Billy, a student at the nearby Alton high school, was nearly grown. Marjorie, now mother to a small son, had expressed some interest in taking over the property. Marjorie's husband Paul, like her two older brothers, was a seafaring Merchant Marine. With the birth of their first child Marjorie had begged him to spend more time at home. Paul had left the service and now worked long hours at the Scott & Williams Knitting Machine Mill in Laconia. The young family needed a home of their own and Marjorie thought she could supplement Paul's smaller factory worker salary with whatever they could produce on the farm.

Barbara too had just begun full-time work. On the surface it seemed not too out of character for the young woman to want to strike off on her own rather than to share the home she had grown up in with her older sister. Barbara wrote to her brothers, telling them that she and a former Gilmanton boy, David, had married quietly in a small ceremony. This was later found to be a lie. Nosy neighbors were assured that the couple was engaged and about to be married shortly.

Tongues may have wagged a little when people realized Barbara had moved in with the parents of her boyfriend. The move might have been a little scandalous by the standards of the 1940s, but it made financial sense and, really, Barbara was just such a hard-working girl it was difficult to find fault with her. With her boyfriend's parents there to act as chaperones it was thought the young couple was just trying to save up money so they could be properly betrothed and married. Only in hindsight would it look more like Barbara had been running away from something, instead of running towards a new future when she left the farm.

It should have been a bright and happy time for the young woman, but a cloud seemed to follow Barbara everywhere she went. Her boyfriend David secured work at the Packard Wool Mill in nearby Ashland. A week after he started Barbara was hired. As at Nockle's her co-workers at the wool mill knew her as a conscientious, proper girl— but they worried for her. They said she popped Aspirin frequently throughout her shifts and she was often found on the machines crying silently. Sometimes the tears would come so hard Barbara would be overwhelmed and would need to leave the machine floor to calm herself. The other women at the Packard Wool Mill assumed she was nervous about her new job and scared of being seated at the large noisy machines in the mill. Shifts were long in the textile mills; the machinery was dangerous. A careless worker could easily lose a finger, a limb, or even their life. Because of the dangers another worker assisted Barbara on the machines until she could get the hang of it. Barbara was polite enough to this co-worker but not overly friendly. She offered no reason for her nervousness and let everyone around her believe she was scared of the machines.

When Lieutenant Commander Charles and Petty Officer Robert had last visited, they had accepted Barbara's explanations easily enough. They had never been given any reason to think their sister would lie to them and Billy had not contradicted any of her stories. But then more and more months passed, first one, then six more months. No word from Sylvester. Not a single telegram to Marjorie. Not one fellow Merchant Marine mentioned seeing him around the Union Hall. No one could recall him being on their crew for some time. Then one day the children's Uncle Earnest received a surprise telegram. Addressed to Sylvester Roberts it was from the Merchant Marines offices, demanding to know why he had not reported for duty in so many months. Earnest contacted his nephews with the news. It was September before the two Roberts brothers could return to the Gilmanton Iron Works farmhouse again. This time they had even more questions and were on a mission to get answers for them.

Asking around town they heard at Nockle's that their father had sent a telegram back in December, this was in direct opposition to what their sister had told them the past April. The brothers went to the family farm to consult with Marjorie. Together they decided Barbara had to be questioned more. Armed with the new information about the telegraph Barbara's brother Charles came demanding answers. He showed up at the Packard Wool Mill in the middle of her three to eleven shift and sat down with her as she combed wool on the drum carding machine. This time Barbara told her brother that she had simply forgotten that she had received the telegram. But, she said, even though she had gotten word promising a Christmas visit, their dad had never shown up. Barbara held firm to the story that since the telegram four days before the Christmas holiday there had been no additional correspondence from Sylvester. But her brother was on high alert and this time he did not let things go as easily as he had in the spring. Sensing there was more to the story than he was being told Charles pressed his sister for more information.

Finally, most likely thinking of whoever had driven Sylvester to the house from the train station, Barbara confessed to something terrible. When her brother led

Barbara from the mill in tears her co-workers assumed he had come to give her news of a death in the family. When they read the newspapers the next day they were as shocked as anyone to what was being reported.

Chapter Seven

I have never sat at my typewriter and written one dishonest thing.
— Grace Metalious, quoted in "The Girl from Peyton Place"

It was already late in the evening on September 5, 1947 when Charles and Marjorie's husband Paul, brought a serene and stylishly dressed Barbara to the police station in Gilmanton. It was not the chic purple dress Laurie Wilkins had seen her in at the farm but was, instead, an equally snappy black wool number that could have come straight out of any of the popular women's magazines on the shelves in Nockle's that month.

But the Barbara Roberts that was led to the Gilmanton Iron Works police station, accompanied by her brother and brother-in-law, was a much different girl than the one townsfolk were used to. There had been a hot dry spell, totally out of season, and the air remained oppressive even as the sun went down. Rain was predicted, not much, but the temperatures had been so unreasonable anything that might break the heat was welcome. Charles explained, briefly, why they were there. Deputy Chief Charles E. Dunleavy took the initial report, eyeing the carefully composed young woman with some skepticism, and then decided this had the potential to be something much bigger than he was normally tasked with handling. Deputy Chief Dunleavy asked the pensive family unit to wait while he called for someone who might be better equipped to decide what to do next. Deputy Chief Dunleavy quickly called Homer Crockett, the Belknap County High sheriff, and County Solicitor William Keller to come down to the station to hear what was being said directly from the Roberts siblings. Briefly Charles told the men that his sister had confessed to murder, earlier at the wool mill.

"In the war I have seen so much," Charles Roberts told the assembled men next. "This is my own sister who has done this, and I had to bring her in to the police. Anyone who is guilty of a crime, relative or not, must be turned over to the authorities. What else is there to do?"[15]

But to the experienced officers Barbara didn't look like a killer. The pretty girl sat calmly as her brother repeated her claims that she had shot her father in the back. She was poised carefully like a model, with her ankles crossed, and wearing the black dress that both made her seem older and younger than her twenty years.

William Keller had worked as a lawyer in the Laconia area for more than ten years before becoming the County Solicitor. Any crime was rare in New Hampshire, murder even more so, but in his job, he had come in contact with all kinds of criminals. At the time of Barbara's confession, he was already dealing with the aftermath of forest fires that had decimated more than twenty-thousand acres of prime New Hampshire woodlands. Keller was also already deep in the midst of another heinous family murder. On August 29, just one short week before the evening confession to Sylvester's death, a local Center Harbor woman named Evelyn Cote had confessed to killing her three-year-old child.

Frustrated that the small boy had soiled his pants Cote had punished the boy by pouring black pepper down his throat in such quantities that he had suffocated and died. Cote had then hitch-hiked with the boy's body to her mother-in-law's house where she called the police, claiming the child had just suddenly keeled over. A quick review by the medical examiner had found the boy's lungs filled with pepper. When police checked the Cote's house, they found the black pepper and a spoon still on the kitchen table. Shown this evidence the boy's mother quickly confessed to what she had done. It was a senseless horrific crime that shook the surrounding lake region towns to their cores. But, as brutish as that crime was, Keller had no trouble envisioning exactly what had happened, he had no doubts about the evil committed by Evelyn Cote. He just didn't feel the same about Barbara Roberts. As much as he couldn't imagine why the girl would lie and make up such a tale, he could not see her as a killer. At one point he even reasoned that the sad sordid tale was just a hallucination, brought on by the unsavory heat, and the isolation of growing up with no parents on a remote New Hampshire farm.

The heat was unrelenting. The interrogation room was a sticky miasma all the men wished to flee. In the middle of it all Barbara Roberts casually smoked a cigarette in her little black dress. She answered when spoken to, in a cultured low voice that seemed at odds with what she was saying. William Keller was so sure of the improbability of the girl's confession that he warned all the men assembled not to jump to any conclusions unless a body was actually found.

At 8:00 pm Sheriff Homer Crockett got tired of all the talk and delay. He had Robert Roberts, Paul Richards, and State Trooper George McKeagney follow him out to the Roberts Farm. They found the little house empty but tidy. Marjorie, described by many who knew her as "highly nervous"[16] and having no delusions about the veracity of what her sister had said, had refused to go to the police station and would not stay on the farm alone. Instead, she had fled to weather the coming storm at her in-law's nearby Alton home.

The three men, led by Sheriff Crockett holding forth a lit torch, walked about the length of a football field to the old barn and attached sheep pen. The four men searched for hours and made several phone calls back to the station to get more precise directions from Barbara. In the middle of all of it Deputy Chief Dunleavy gave the confessed killer another cigarette and asked if she was hungry. Barbara politely told him she wasn't, but she would be very grateful for a cup of coffee. The police station didn't have its own coffee maker, so Officer Clyde Beaulieu was sent to Earl's Diner to pick up a cup to go. The call came in around ten o'clock. Sylvester Roberts had finally been found. Beneath the loose floorboards of the sheep pen, just as Barbara had described, the white bones of her father gleamed beneath the flames of the torch.

Chapter Eight

"Indian summer is like a woman. Ripe, hotly passionate, but fickle, she comes and goes as she pleases so that one is never sure whether she will come at all, nor for how long she will stay."
— Grace Metalious, "Peyton Place"

It was not until the bones, picked clean of every scrap of flesh, were found that Barbara showed the first small signs of nervousness. In the stuffy little interrogation room, made that much smaller by the presence of her brother Charles, William Keller, and the two officers she began to idly open and close the gold clasp on her smart black purse. Click, Click, Click. The buckle, crafted from her initials BER, opened. The buckle shut. Once or twice, she rooted half-heartedly around in its dark depths but never seemed to find what she was looking for. The body now giving credence to her story Barbara was asked to begin her confession again. She did as she was asked, still speaking calmly, but talking so quietly that the stagnant air seemed to suffocate the words as they fell from her perfectly made-up rosy lips.

"As he came up the walk, he was raving . . . "

Barbara Roberts told it all: the telegram, the broken-down car, and the deep, deep anger of her father. She said she was alone in the house when she heard her father raging around outside of it. She lingered over the laundry, wishing to be somewhere, anywhere but where she was. Her father tried the side door to the kitchen and found it locked, which only enraged him more. She could hear him crunching through the remains of the ice-crusted snow as he made his way to the front door. Working up her courage to confront him she was en route to unlock the door when, she said, Sylvester charged straight into the house.

He found her by the kitchen door, frozen with fear, and he said nothing as he gripped her fiercely by the throat. She was stunned, as much by the coldness of his hands as she was by the deathly tight grip of them. Flailing wildly, she got in one good smack that made him briefly let her go. Sylvester stumbled into the kitchen, turning on lights as he went and still swearing up a storm. Barbara remembered her father's promise to kill her if she ever neglected to pick him up at the train station. And that's when she said she shot him: one deadly accurate time, right in the center of his back. Barbara, saying that a loaded rifle was always kept in the dining room next to the kitchen door along with a pistol that was kept in a drawer by the sink, did not know which gun she had used to kill him.

With the body found and Barbara continuing to insist that she had killed Sylvester, entirely on her own and unbeknownst to anyone else, there was nothing left to be done that night but to write down the confession, exactly as she told it, and to have her sign her name to it:

> "My name is Barbara Roberts. I live with [my boyfriend's mother] at Ashland. I understand that I do not have to talk and that anything I say may be used against me. This statement is made voluntarily without any promise having been made.
>
> I shot my father, Sylvester Roberts, last December at our home in Gilmanton Iron Works. This happened December 23, 1946 at 6 p.m. I shot him with a gun that was at the house. It was his gun; I don't know what caliber it was. After I shot him, I

> dragged him into the barn myself and put him into the cellar under the sheep pen. There was nobody there when all this happened. I never told anybody about this until I told my brother today (Sept. 5)"[17]

"I think he was dead right away," Barbara said to the stunned room, coolly finishing her confession.[18]

William Keller considered what she had said. Even with the skeleton and the young girl in front of him spelling out in precise, if quiet, detail just how the body had gotten beneath the sheep pen floorboards he could not see it clearly in his mind's eye. The timeworn though well-kept farmhouse kitchen, the slim girl in front of him holding the smoking rifle, and her father, still dressed in his Merchant Marine's uniform, laying prone on the wood floor. None of it seemed possible. It was then that he asked the question he always asked— to Evelyn Cote who poured black pepper down her toddler's throat over potty training, to the Laconia townies who got too rowdy at the local bars. It was the question that they always seemed to get around to in this little interrogation room, hardly more than a closet and feeling like an oven on this dry September evening.

"And then what did you do? What happened next?"

Barbara seems to have blacked out for a while. Not as emotionless as she seemed the night of her confession, she said she lost at least an hour after the shooting. After this blank hour where it seemed that she had done nothing, she explained that she had no choice but to find some place to conceal the body. Insisting that she was alone and that no one was the wiser to what she had done, Barbara said she threw a sheet over her father's body. She then half carried, half dragged, the literal dead weight of her slain father through the kitchen, across the fields, and through the barn into the sheep pen. Even two days before Christmas, on one of the coldest nights of the year, in sharp contrast to when she would tell her story, the ground there remained unfrozen.

The heat of the sheep and the constant rat a tat tat of their small hoofed feet across the floorboards kept the ground as soft as any she was going to find on the property that time of year.

Rooting around Barbara was able to pull up some loose floorboards in the pen. There, recessed in shadow was a small space of roughly eighteen inches between the cold ground and the softly rotting wooden floor. Somehow, she was able to push, pull and shove her father's rapidly stiffening body into that space. It made a sad grave where Sylvester would lie, undisturbed, for nine months.

Keller was suspicious from the start. Even if he could wrap his head around the girl killing her own father, he just couldn't see her having the wherewithal to move the body so far on her own. Other people in Gilmanton Iron Works would have the same issue. Many believed that Billy had to have done the deed. If he was not the true killer of Sylvester Roberts, at the very least, he must have helped his sister hide the body.

"That night after the shooting I washed some blood off the kitchen floor," Barbara told the hushed lawmen, adding that the kitchen door had also been damaged and broken glass needed to be swept up as well.[19]

Keller looked at the young woman in front of him, the murderess that in a few days' time newspapers would describe as "a lady in every way."[20] It was then that he asked the next question that, inevitably, the room always heard. Because after hearing that a crime had been committed what came next was the question everyone always wanted to know.

"Why? Why did you *really* do it?"

Chapter Nine

In the big city there are more interesting things to do than be overly concerned with your neighbor.
— Grace Metalious, in an interview

Long before the advent of the twenty-four-hour news cycle or the relentless share-ability of news articles on the internet the murder of Sylvester Roberts could be said to have gone viral. From the first morning after the body was found Barbara was a sensation. Newspapers around the country breathlessly reported on the confession made by his daughter, usually called the "Girl Slayer" by media sources that were from away but always just "Barbara" to the local newspaper headline writers. The idea of a daughter killing her father was interesting enough on its own. But add in that the murderer was young and pretty and you had a recipe for newspaper sales that could not be topped.

While Gilmanton Iron Works may have seemed tucked away in the middle of nowhere it is really only eighteen miles from New Hampshire's capital, Concord, and only a few more to Manchester, the state's largest city. The combination of murder, a desirable young lady killer, and the hint that there might be a deeper scandal behind it all was more than enough to make the case a sensation. Every aspect of Barbara's life, from her confession to the impending trial were covered in detail by New England newspapers. Nearly all of the articles about the crime described, in-depth, what

Barbara looked like and what she wore. She never wore just a dress. It was always a short-sleeve black dress "which lends itself so well to collars and costume jewelry."[21] Every aspect of her appearance was remarked upon, from the combs she wore in her hair to her weight, helpfully estimated by one paper to be 130 pounds.

The local Lakes Region newspaper was *The Laconia Evening Citizen*, where Laurie Wilkins was a staff writer. Although Laconia was the closest thing to a real city center in the Lakes area in the 1940s the paper had the kind of chatty, feel-good reporting you would expect to see from the weekly edition in a much smaller town. Much of the paper was filled with news of sales being held in local shops, and advertisements for snake oil promising the cheap and easy removal of pin worms, back pain, and what the ads described winkingly as 'periodic' female weakness and nervousness. The majority of the pages were given over to coverage of local sports. Photographs of local brides, all in the requisite frothy white dress, often made the front page. World news was limited to rehashing the Royal Wedding of Queen Elizabeth and Prince Philip at Westminster Abbey in England. In the fall of 1947 the big topic of conversation in the *Laconia Evening Citizen* was an upcoming agricultural fair at which, readers were told, a female police officer would be joining the ranks for the first time to help with crowd control and safety. The headlines generated by Sylvester Roberts' murder and the extra-large photographs of his murderous daughter were glaringly conspicuous among this more innocuous reading.

Some of the earliest reports of the murder mentioned Sylvester's temper and his threat to kill Barbara if she ever missed picking him up from the train station. But all of them worked in a quote from Charles Roberts about the thousands of dollars he said the brothers, and his father, had sent to Barbara over the years they were at sea. One paper reported that what should have been a full bank account held in the girl's name to cover household expenses had a balance of just six cents when she confessed to murder. Barbara's brothers were also quoted as saying that jewelry belonging to their mother, which should have been in the Gilmanton home, was missing. None of the papers came right out and said it, but the inference was that the murder had something to do with money. That perhaps Sylvester had been so angry not because he had to walk home from the train station but because he had discovered the missing rings and money. Or maybe Barbara had killed him not out of self-defense but because she was trying to conceal the smaller crime of theft.

There is a true unsung hero in the case of Barbara Roberts, a newspaperman by the name of Ben Bradlee. Long before serving as editor of *The Washington Post,* befriending John F. Kennedy, or green-lighting the publication of The Pentagon Papers during the Watergate scandal Ben Bradlee was a recent Naval veteran in need of a job. He had come from an aristocratic Boston family that had, during the Great Depression, fallen on hard times. Bradlee had an interest in journalism and even some small experience. At the age of 15 he had worked for $5 a week at the *Beverly Evening Times* in Beverly, Massachusetts. A former classmate got him a job for a fledging paper called *The New Hampshire Sunday News.* This was a once-a-week edition of 64 pages located out of Manchester, New Hampshire. Ben Bradlee helped start the paper and would be one of just seven staffers for the length of the paper's run.

The *New Hampshire Sunday News* was a progressive publication for its time. While it shared the same fascination with wedding announcements and local sports as *The Laconia Evening Citizen,* under Bradlee's direction the paper also exposed terrible conditions at the (very not politically correctly named) Laconia State School for the Feebleminded (George Metalious would teach at the school years later in the early start of his educational career). It also demanded justice in crimes against women like the murder of Ruth

McGurk, which remains unsolved to this day, and Naomi Hall. While the paper was not completely immune from the misogyny of the day, a 'Woman of the Week' column tended to focus on housewives of local politicians and it showed a preoccupation with the numbers of divorced women, the paper also alerted readers to the fact that literal ball and chains were still being used in New Hampshire prisons to restrain prisoners.

Bradlee would work for the *New Hampshire Sunday News* for just two years before it was bought out by its biggest competition, the *Manchester Union-Leader*. At that point the struggling journalist once again turned to friends for help finding a new job. He soon began work as a reporter for *The Washington Post*. In time he become managing editor and then executive editor for the prestigious paper. He would be awarded many times over the work he did there, earning everything from a Golden Plate Award from the American Academy of Achievement to a Walter Cronkite Award for Excellence in Journalism. In 2013 President Barack Obama would award Ben Bradlee a Presidential Medal of Freedom. In his memoir, *A Good Life,* Bradlee would credit his later success to some of his early journalistic pursuits in New England, writing, "I learned a vital lesson: people will talk if they feel comfortable."

But in 1947 he was just a reporter for a struggling paper that was only a few months from being bought out. Bradlee made a point to stay on top of what was happening statewide and, really, there was no bigger case in New Hampshire than the Roberts case. Bradlee decided to dig deeper into the story than most of the other papers of the day were. Instead of simply printing an alluring photo of the young murderess with her confession as many other papers did Ben Bradlee took a fearless deep dive into the dysfunctional dynamics of the Roberts family. Bradlee not only had staff pursue the reasons behind Barbara's crime relentlessly, but he was also brave enough to publish the things they found in far more graphic language than the other newspapers of the day would be comfortable doing. This type of aggressive reporting mixed with compelling human stories would become a hallmark of Ben Bradlee's career. In short order the reporting done swayed public opinion, making readers much more sympathetic to the accused killer than to her victim.

Because that night in the Gilmanton Police station Barbara had not just confessed to the murder of her father. After a lifetime of silence, she had finally admitted to years of sexual abuse that had begun after the death of her mother, starting when the girl was just thirteen years old. In her hushed emotionless voice Barbara shared harrowing memories of her father's outrageous temper and the extreme abuse she had suffered at his hands. Barbara said she had lived in terror of his temper for most of her life.

"The reason I shot my father," Barbara insisted, "was because I was afraid, he would kill me. He had beaten me up before. When we were little kids that's all he did. When I was thirteen years old my father tied me in the bed and abused me. He threatened me so there was nothing I could do."[22]

Chapter Ten

"He had two faces. One he showed the neighbors and the other he showed at home.
— An anonymous Gilmanton Iron Works resident, to *The Laconia Evening Evening Citizen*, September 12, 1947

There is a common belief held by many people today that in days gone past sexual abuse was not discussed. Some believe that it was not even seen rightfully as a crime. While some of the social mores and niceties surrounding these kinds of crimes have progressed over the years it is a complete misconception to think that the types of things Barbara Roberts said drove her to kill her father would not be seen as a crime or would be glossed over. The work done by Ben Bradlee definitely went far in sharing the motivations behind the crime but the *New Hampshire Sunday News* was not the only paper that would report the full extent of Barbara's confession.

The Lowell Sun, headquartered in a major mill city seventy miles south of Gilmanton, covered the Roberts case as closely as the local Lakes Region papers did. *The Lowell Sun* published a lengthy front-page article that included most of Barbara's signed and written confession. They had no problem quoting her about being tied to the bed at age thirteen though they stuck to the word "abuse" rather than specify anything sexual. Readers could do the work themselves to infer what the quote really meant.

Elsewhere on that front page that same day, tucked in next to a notice about a new feature called "As We Live," written by a female psychologist that would help women get answers to the "perplexing problems of everyday life" like the psychology of dress and modern child-rearing, was a small notice about a local man who had been found guilty of assault and battery. The three-inch-long article explained that a ten-year-old girl had testified in a closed session in the judge's chambers about being assaulted one afternoon after entering the general store owned by the defendant. The word sex is never used in the scant article but in this matter too readers could deduce just what kind of crime had been committed against the pre-pubescent Lowell girl.

In fact, the many articles printed nationwide about Barbara Roberts and the New Hampshire slaying of her father appeared side by side with many stories of crimes against women. One article, given just as much space as one about Barbara Roberts's trial reported a $30 fine that had been levied against a 22-year-old man who had pulled an unwilling woman into the yard of Lowell's Butler School.[23] Men in a passing vehicle saw the woman's distress and came to her aid. In another article a woman was brought up on charges that she drowned her illegitimate daughter, born while her husband was stationed in New Jersey, and that she then concealed the small body in the cellar of her home. The woman was quoted, saying she had been attacked in an automobile by two men nine months before the birth of the child.[24] In this instance too readers could do the math as to what kind of attack had taken place. In another instance a "petite and shapely" 18-year-old court stenographer was abducted after a robbery attempt and held for six hours in a wild car ride with her increasingly drunk captor.[25] The papers plainly reported that the lucky woman had not been molested while held captive.

However, there was one story whose headlines jostled those of the Roberts family on the front pages of New

England's newspapers that included the word sex quite freely. "Seven-Year-Old Girl Victim of Lawrence Sex Slayer" blared one headline in *The Lowell Sun* in inch high letters. Just three days after Barbara Roberts gave her emotionless confession the body of Louise Ann Kurpiel had been found, nude, on the banks of the Merrimack River with a crushed skull. The body was just a few hundred feet from the Joseph W. Casey Bridge, the site of a homeless encampment, in Lawrence, Massachusetts by an unnamed man whom the police described as someone familiar to the area. Near the small, battered body was a large rock, covered in the girl's blood and bone fragments from her skull. Drag marks near the body suggested that whoever had killed her had attempted to throw the body into the Merrimack before abandoning it in plain view on the banks of that same river. "Police," *The Lowell Sun* reported, "are of the opinion that she was the victim of a sex fiend."[26]

An alarm had been raised the evening before when Louise failed to return home from a friend's house. Acting quickly, a group of over one hundred friends, family, and neighbors were combing the streets for her within the hour. She wasn't found until the next morning and by then it was already far too late. The coroner estimated that she had been bludgeoned with the rock around 9:00 p.m. the previous evening, probably around the same time concerned residents had gathered en mass to look for her.

The same day the body was discovered the police found a witness, possibly the last person outside of her killer to have seen Louise alive. The witness had seen the little girl walking hand in hand with a man the previous evening, around 7:00 p.m. At 8:30 p.m. he was seen again, by the same witness and others, covered in blood and without the little girl.

The police quickly deduced that the man was twenty-one-year-old Vincent Delle Chiaie. He had been in the area that same day attending a wedding where he became, according to witnesses, increasingly intoxicated. The cops were able to immediately track him down in Franklin, New Hampshire, where he had fled after dropping his bloody clothes in plain sight in his apartment. Vincent said he remembered meeting Louise but that he was so drunk after the wedding that the rest of the afternoon and evening were a complete blank. Later he would recant and sign a confession saying he had hit Louise with a rock to silence her screams when we tried to rape her. Delle Chiaie's mother said his mind had come undone after serving in the war. Delle Chiaie would, in time, be sentenced to death in the electric chair for the murder of Louise Kurpiel, though that punishment would be commuted to life in prison in 1949, and then commuted again to offer the possibility of parole in 1974. And all that in spite of a daring, though short-lived, 1960 escape from prison.

If it seems strange that the newspapers would be so willing to write about the rape of a child while couching the molestation of Barbara Roberts in less graphic terms like "sordid details" and "unhappy childhood,"[27] one has to consider the other things written about the young Gilmanton Iron Works woman. In the many newspaper articles written about the case at the time Barbara is described as a "pretty New Hampshire girl,"[28] "the attractive Gilmanton Iron Works girl"[29] a "lady-like girl, pretty and popular"[30] and "comely."[31] The press, and the titillated residents of New England who closely followed the case, were as taken with the stylishly dressed and always carefully composed murderer as William Keller had been. The police fed fuel to the flames when they told the press the confessed killer, a "comely brunette,"[32] was "very pretty and lady-like."[33] One paper, before commenting on her clothing choices, lamented that the "girl from the tiny village farm and her counterpart in the city can no longer be told apart."[34]

Even though the abuse she had suffered at her father's hands had begun when she was only a few years older than Louise Kurpiel readers of the region's newspapers saw her confession printed alongside the photo of her as she was at the time— a young woman, eyes downcast, with a hand lingeringly touching her mouth as if she were daydreaming. It was not so much that the public didn't believe Barbara, just that she did not make quite as clear a victim as Louise Kurpiel made.

Overall, there was surprisingly little disbelief in Barbara's stories of growing up under her father's wrathful temper. Frank Dowst, the Police Chief Barbara had tried to turn to for help the night of the murder, was one of the people who was quick to come to Barbara's defense. Dowst shared with the press the now haunting words Barbara had spoken a year before the body had been found— "You have no idea of the kind of life I lead when my father is home." The phrase had suddenly taken on a much clearer, and darker, meaning than he had first supposed. Back that spring several Gilmanton residents had reported to Dowst about Barbara's near frantic search for him. When he had met her on the street and asked why she had been looking for him the girl had been evasive.

"I did want to see you a while ago," Barbara had told him, months before anyone would learn of the murder she had committed. "But I guess I don't need you now."[35]

Frank Dowst would always wonder if Barbara had been looking for him to confess her crime. Others speculated that she would not have killed Sylvester if only she had been able to turn to Dowst for help that evening.

Surprisingly one of the few early dissenters to Barbara's confession was her oldest brother, Charles. He told the police that while his father did have a temper he was as quick to cool down as he was to fire up. When instances of incest were mentioned at Barbara's arraignment Charles was as stunned as anyone in the courtroom and buried his head in his hands. But then William spoke up about the abuse he had witnessed while Charles was out at sea. And then, even more damningly, the oldest Roberts sister Marjorie shared her own stories of sexual abuse at the hands of Sylvester.

Marjorie Roberts also shared her experiences with Bradlee's *New Hampshire Sunday News*, swearing she would testify to her father's Jekyll and Hyde nature and backing up Barbara's stories of sexual abuse.

"We will help Barbara all we can, it was terrible and I hate to even think about it," Marjorie told the *New Hampshire Sunday News*, speaking for her siblings and husband Paul. "I know what Barbara went through and I am sure any decent man on a jury couldn't convict her."[36]

Popular opinion was, in many ways, on Barbara's side even if the same public salivated at the salacious details of the crime printed in the papers. The revelations about Sylvester's treatment of his children, in particular his two daughters, made the young woman an extremely sympathetic figure. In the eyes of many what Barbara Roberts did was seen as self-defense. Besides the history of abuse the angry promise of "I'll kill you" could be taken quite literally especially when paired with angry, icy hands around a girl's slender throat. But there were others who could, and would, point out that Sylvester had been shot in the back as he was walking away from his daughter.

If readers were quick to accept the idea that a father could force his daughters into incestuous acts they were also just as quick to believe that the "perfect lady,"[37] as a supervisor at the prison she was held at while awaiting trial described her, could also be a deadly killer. Because just as the newspaper articles that shared space with the Barbara Roberts story reported on crimes against women, there was no shortage of crimes being reported on that were committed by women. Barbara appeared in the pages of *The Atlanta Constitution* right next to a "red-haired wife" who had enlisted the help of two teenaged boys in the shooting death of her husband.[38] Add in the murder of Evelyn Cote's little boy and we can see that the people of the 1940s were well aware that women were not always the kinder, gentler sex.

Chapter Eleven

Which is more cruel? Isolation, or the constant prying and lack of privacy you have in a small town, where people love digging into each other's closets?
— Grace Metalious, in an interview

Barbara was arraigned the morning after her late-night confession on September 6, 1947 at the Laconia Municipal Court. She had no lawyer to represent her, but her brother Charles stayed close by her side. Just as Barbara had once stepped up and taken over the parenting role for her brother Billy, Charles now did the same for her. He was, like all the Roberts, slightly built but well put together. He had a fresh-faced All-American look that was at odds with the sordid situation the family now found themselves in. During the coming months he would fully take over responsibilities as head of the household. Charles would become a spokesman of sorts for the family when dealing with the press and arranging Barbara's legal affairs. But the morning of the arraignment he looked lost. The previous day had been a shocking one, and it had run late into the night. Still his suit was nicely pressed and his concern for his sister's well-being was evident to everyone in the courtroom.

Judge Harry E. Trapp called the court to order an hour later than originally scheduled and tensions were running extra high in the courtroom with the unexpected delay. This was well before the days of courtroom television and few people realized legal proceedings could be a spectator sport. So, there were only a few people in the room who were not there to offer some kind of statement about the murder of Sylvester Roberts. Those who were not associated with the case watched Barbara with some surprise and obvious curiosity, paying close attention to the young woman behind the defendant's table. They said she gave no visible reaction when the full charges were read.

William Keller read her signed confession into the record while Barbara sat impassively in the defendant's chair. She could have been sitting at the drum carder in the wool mill for all the interest she showed the proceedings. Then Sheriff Crockett took the stand. As he described the finding of the gleaming white skeleton of Sylvester Roberts, tucked beneath the loose floorboards of the sheep pen Barbara placed her slim white hands, surprisingly youthful for a girl who had worked so hard for so many years at farm work and in the mills, over her eyes. It was the only emotion she showed during the entire spectacle.

Next came the Belknap County Medical Referee to testify. Earl J. Gage told the court he had been called out to the Roberts' farm around midnight the night before. He had examined the bones but said there was so little left of the body he would not even be able to conduct a full autopsy. Mr. Gage said the bones had been packed up and sent to the Wilkinson Funeral Home, pending investigation. They would sit there for months, unclaimed by the family, before finally being buried far off in Salem, Massachusetts. Mr. Gage mused that because Barbara had sold off all the sheep the barn and attached pen got little use, which had further helped to conceal the body since no one would have been present to detect the smell of decomposition. He said with so little evidence to be gleaned from the fully decomposed corpse any further answers would have to be discovered with William Keller's investigative skills. Mr. Keller later tried to get the State Pathologist, Ralph Miller, to look over the bones. Forensic examination was not what it is now. The state would have to put out a public appeal to find any other possible expert to assist in a future examination.

Charles Roberts, although there in a show of support for his younger sibling, was also called to take the stand and speak against her. With little prompting he went over the sequence of events that led to him confronting his sister at the wool mill the day before, and then ended in her confession.

"I must tell you something," Charles quoted his sister as saying. "I killed our father."[39]

Finally, Barbara Roberts was called on to speak. Still dressed in the same black dress as she had worn to the police station the night before Barbara, speaking in a whisper that could barely be heard, tried to enter a plea of guilty. The judge stopped her, telling her she had to say not guilty at this point in the process. He warned her that if she continued down this path, she would be sentenced to at least thirty years in prison. After some back and forth between them Barbara was finally convinced to declare herself not guilty of the crime of killing her father Sylvester Robert, aged 52, on December 23, 1946.

"She seemed like in a daze," Allan J. Ayre, the photographer who captured the pensive photo of Barbara that would be published in papers across the country in the coming months, said of her behavior in court that day. "It was like she was waiting for a dentist appointment."[40]

After the conclusion of the arraignment, she was sent to the Belknap County Farm to await trial. After leaving the courthouse the enormity of the past few days finally hit her and Barbara's preternatural calm began to crack.

Charles Roberts quickly found a local lawyer to take up the case defending his sister. Luckily this lawyer happened to share his offices with a medical doctor, who was also his sister. The sister, Dr. M. Alice Normandin, was called out to the Belknap County Farm at 11:30 the day after the arraignment for assistance when the Superintendent and his wife reported the prisoner was in a “highly nervous condition”[41] and needed immediate assistance.

Chapter Twelve

I've never been able to profit from experience. I find myself, time after time, thinking, 'Never mind what happened before, tomorrow will be better.'
— Grace Metalious

The Belknap County Farm was not expressly a prison, although it was sometimes used that way, and many would refer to it as the county jail. Modern-day readers might know this kind of establishment better as an almshouse, a working farm, or a poor house. Many may have never heard of any of these terms at all. At best some might recall this exchange from the Charles Dickens' classic *A Christmas Carol* when two gentlemen approach Ebenezer Scrooge about donating to the poor:

> "Are there no prisons?" asks Scrooge. . . "And the Union workhouses? "Are they still in operation?"
>
> "I wish to be left alone," said Scrooge. "Since you ask me what I wish, gentlemen, that is my answer. I don't make merry myself at Christmas and I can't afford to make idle people merry. I help to support the establishments I have mentioned: they cost enough: and those who are badly off must go there."
>
> "Many can't go there; and many would rather die."

> "If they would rather die," said Scrooge, "they had better do it, and decrease the surplus population."

The poor and indigent, anyone who could not pay their bills or survive on their own often had no other recourse but to go live and work at an almshouse. It was not necessarily meant to be a punishment. Local residents saw it as their way of creating work and care for people who would not otherwise have it— the mentally ill, the developmentally or physically disabled; anyone who did not have family able or willing to care for them could end up at the poor farm. But the fact that so many people were sent unwillingly, and often by the legal system, paints the practice in a slightly different light. You could be sent to the poorhouse, by the courts and not by choice, for not being able to pay off your debts or if you had racked up legal fees that you couldn't cover.

Pre-1800s people in this position would have been sent to debtor's prisons. At the Federal level these institutions were outlawed in the United States in 1833. While states could still choose to operate debtors' prisons most switched to the use of a poorhouse, which was seen as being more humane, even if they more or less served the same purpose in more or less the same sort of way. Once you were sent to the workhouse, as the name implies, you would be put to work. Everyone was expected to do some sort of job, in as much as their age and health would allow. But in many places residents wouldn't be paid for the work they did, so if they had been sent to the workhouse for an unpaid debt, they would never really have a way to work their way out of the system.

The Belknap County Farm, located in Laconia, began life in 1835 as a mental institution. A fire would destroy the original structure in 1871. The county decided to rebuild, this time as a large white two-story farmhouse, and expanded its outreach to house "the insane, the poor, the infirm, as well as people who had committed criminal acts." Further reform would come about in the early 1900s when it was decided that the infirm and disabled could be victimized by some of the more career criminals being sent there. Criminals could still be sent to the farm, but it was usually reserved for non-violent offenders.

By the time Barbara Roberts took up residence there Belknap County Farm was like many of the workhouses that flourished in New England through the 1900s. They were, much like during its start as a mental institution, a place of last resort for most residents. While it was not common by the 1940s that the poor farm would be used as a holding place for prisoners as we see in the case of Barbara Roberts it wasn't unheard of. New Hampshire lacked formal facilities for female prisoners and it helped that public opinion was very much in the young mill worker's favor. There is not much evidence that there was any kind of outcry or concern for the other residents when she went to spend her time at the poor farm instead of a traditional prison. This might have been helped by the fact that the terms 'county farm,' 'county workhouse,' and 'county prison' were all used freely and interchangeably. Many would not realize that Barbara was not in a more secure traditional facility. Little concern was paid to the state's lack of facilities for its female prisoners.

As far as poor farms went, Belknap County Farm was not the worst place someone could end up. The accommodations were simple and sparse, but the work was no worse than in many places and was quite a bit better than some. Since the beginning the farm had been overseen by husband-and-wife teams who not only saw to the needs of the residents at the farm but lived and worked there themselves. One 1835 resident, recorded only as Rebecca, entered the farm at age 33. She would remain a resident until she passed away at age 85. This might be because she had no other option: she may have needed medical or mental health care and it was the only place that could provide it for her, but it could also be because the conditions were decent enough that she had chosen to stay fifty-two years.

In the 1940s, as since the farm's start, the residents and buildings were overseen by a Superintendent named Leon Flanders and his wife. Superintendent Flanders took his duties seriously, restricting the visitors for Barbara as he had been directed by the state, but he was also a kind and generous man. He and his wife were sympathetic to Barbara, a hardworking girl who was probably an asset for the farm work.

"Barbara is a perfect lady," he would tell *The Laconia Evening Citizen* in 1947. "She co-operated with us to the letter while she was with us and never gave Mrs. Flanders or myself a bit of trouble."[42]

At the Belknap County Farm residents raised livestock, sold lumber, and produced crops for their own consumption or trade— overall life would not have been all that different for Barbara than it had been on her own family farm. If anything, she may have found the work a reprieve from farm life as things at the Belknap County Farm were split traditionally along gender lines. As a woman Barbara would have been more likely to be found baking in the kitchen or mending the laundry of the other residents than slaughtering livestock as she had done for many years on her own. During the time Barbara was at the farm this livestock included at least dairy cows, it is unclear if they had any sheep. It is also unknown if anyone ever saw any irony in sending the girl who had confessed to a "Sheep Pen Murder" to go live on a farm while she awaited trial.

Chapter Thirteen

No matter what crime you commit you can always go on living in a small town.
— Grace Metalious

After the arraignment ended Charles knew he had to get legal counsel for his sister. No one in their family had ever been in any real trouble before. If the simple arraignment had proven anything to him, it was that they were all in way over their heads. That same afternoon Charles hired the Normandin law firm in Laconia, New Hampshire to represent Barbara. The Normandin law firm was truly a family business. F.E Normandin had started the law firm with his brother in 1914, sharing the rented law offices with their sister Alice, a medical doctor. By the time of the Roberts case the founding partners had been joined by a nephew, F. A. Normandin, who would also help in Barbara's defense. However, as prestigious as the firm was in the Lakes Region, they did not normally take on criminal cases.

Attorney Normandin visited Barbara often at the county farm, and later in the state hospital in Concord, often with her brother Charles in attendance. She was not allowed visitors otherwise. Charles had taken time off from his job as a Merchant Marine in order to ensure he was in Gilmanton to support his sister through the murder trial. Robert Roberts also extended his furlough so he could be there for the family, no matter how long the case took. Robert was the less outgoing of the brothers and was happy to let Charles, as the oldest, take over much of the decision-making. The two brothers, after years of separation at sea, had suddenly found themselves together again as they were as boys, but for the time living at the home of their Uncle Charles.

Attorney Normandin gave periodic updates to the media about Barbara's health and mental state. When asked for details about the case he would tell reporters that William Keller was investigating, and all the evidence would come out at trial. To the press Mr. Normandin always seemed confident that his client would walk away free.

"Barbara has a justifiable and legal defense," he said repeatedly when pressed by members of the media with questions about the girl's guilt or possible punishment.[43]

While Attorney Normandin met with Barbara and tried to craft a defense William Keller was busily collecting whatever evidence could be found to ensure the young woman was convicted. The day after the arraignment he was back at the Gilmanton Iron Works farmhouse trying to piece together everything that had happened there ten months previous. With help from the deputy sheriffs and State Trooper McKeagney, who had been on hand for the discovery of the victim's bones the night of Barbara's confession, he scoured the kitchen for anything that could be presented to a jury. The farmhouse door, showing evidence of damage from bullet holes, was removed and sent to the State Police headquarters in Concord. But what the men most wanted to find was any kind of proof that Barbara really could have moved the body of her father all the way out to the barn on her own.

With so little evidence left to be gathered anything linked to the crime had to be fully explored. When the Medical Referee Dr. Gage could not perform an autopsy on what remained of Sylvester Roberts a call was put out for expert assistance. After weeks of searching Dr. Richard Ford, an Assistant Professor of Legal Medicine at Harvard Medical

School, was finally called to come out and offer any opinion he might have on the remains.

The police decided to put the public's attention to the case to work. Other calls for assistance with the case were also publicized. Police searched far and wide for an unnamed Alton man they thought might have some information to share. It may have been a friend or former boyfriend of Barbara. Her current beau, either her boyfriend or fiancée depending on who was telling the news, was called in to give a statement the afternoon after the arraignment. He spent only a brief time with the police before they let him go.

Billy Roberts did not get such a brief period of questioning. After the police spent several hours talking to the sixteen-year-old boy they decided to hold him. Officers brought the scared, undersized high school student to Juvenile Court to meet privately with a judge. On September 9th Deputy Sheriff Herman Olsen, the same deputy sheriff who had led Barbara Robert into court just days earlier, led her sixteen-year-old brother Billy into the judge's chambers. Also in the chambers for this closed-door meeting were Charles Roberts, William Keller, High Sheriff Crockett, Deputy Sheriffs Olsen and Fred Elliott, and Barbara's lawyer F.E. Normandin. State Trooper George McKeagney stood on the steps of the juvenile court to keep the press out. He cautioned every photographer in the crowd that they should not try to take any pictures of Billy as he walked between the court and the car that drove him there.

After an hour-long closed-door meeting Judge Trapp reluctantly gave a statement to the press:

> "The County Solicitor and Attorney F.E. Normandin have suggested I make a statement. Proceedings were held in Juvenile Court, September 9, in which William Roberts was involved in connection with the death of Sylvester Roberts.

> No inferences or conclusions are to be drawn from these proceedings. Juvenile Court matters are secret, according to our New Hampshire law, unless divulged by the consent of the court. The only matter that the court and the county solicitor feel is proper to divulge at this time is that William Roberts was in Juvenile Court in connection with the investigation as previously stated. He was represented by Attorney F.E. Normandin.
>
> All persons present have been cautioned by the court to give no information with connection with the hearing." [44]

Judge Trapp's warning, and the intimidating presence of the State Trooper, worked. While plenty of papers ran the news that Billy had been in court that day not a single one ran any photos of the boy with those articles.

Although Judge Trapp said no conclusion should be drawn from Billy's day in court it was hard for people to not make assumptions. While the boy had been living with family members after Barbara was taken away, the court decided he should be kept in state custody after the closed-door hearing. Billy was sent to Manchester, where the state kept what was known as the State Industrial School.

This facility had been created in 1855 as a reformatory for minor children. The original building had once been a farm owned by Revolutionary War hero General John Stark. At its onset the State Industrial School functioned more or less the same as the Belknap County Farm. Boys were sent there and were expected to learn better behavior through simple living and hard labor. In 1865 the original farm burned to the ground. Shortly after the building burned a second building where the inmates (at the State Industrial School all the children were known as inmates, not residents as at the county farms) had been moved to also burned. While no cause was listed for either fire it seems safe to say they were probably both caused by a bit of arson from one of the children sent to live there.

Over time a new facility was built and with it the state added more than just agricultural pursuits to the options offered there. In 1914 a woodworking shop had been added and, thanks to a donation of instruments from a Manchester native, the boys were encouraged to learn music. Masonry was taught to inmates and a poultry processing facility had been in use since the early 1900s. Inmates were not always male; a small number of girls would be remanded to the care of the State Industrial School, but only very, very few. While thousands of boys had come in and out of the facility over the years only around a hundred girls had been admitted. A 1915 report from the Industrial School supervisor broke down the offenses that could lead children to be sent to the school under his care. Not all of them were purely criminal. While larceny was listed as the most common offense, so was 'stubbornness.' Stubbornness was actually the second most common cause listed for male inmates and it was number one for girls. The same year as the 1915 report was released three girls were also placed into the State Industrial School's care because of fornication, though no boys seemed to have been sent for the same offense.

When children were sent to the State Industrial School it was usually after being convicted of a crime. Sometimes homeless teenagers were sent to the school, but Billy had family that was willing to take him in. It was far less common for inmates to be sent there while in a kind of limbo status like Billy Roberts was. Regardless of the crime they had been convicted of, once a child walked through the doors, they were considered inmates until they turned 21 years of age. A girl suspected of stubbornness would serve just as long an amount of time as a boy who had assaulted someone violently. Well-behaved inmates could be paroled at the age of 16 but only if they were enrolled in school or had jobs. They also had to prove they had a living arrangement that the state deemed as proper. These parolees would be checked on randomly throughout their time outside the facility until they too turned 21. Parolees who offended while on the outside or whose home situation was not up to the moral code of whoever was checking on them would be sent back to the State Industrial School, and they would not get another chance to leave again until they were of age.

Attorney Normandin checked in on Billy often during the months after his first court appearance. He found the boy in good spirits. He told the Roberts family that he often found Billy at work in the masonry building, cleaning bricks that would then be used to help maintain the school's buildings or that would be sold by the state to help offset the cost of the boy's care.

Chapter Fourteen

She was, in her own way, an ultra-compassionate woman almost to her own destruction.
— George Metalious, talking about his wife Grace.

County Solicitor William Keller, like the Attorneys Normandin, was also repeatedly approached by the press, but he never had much to tell them. The word had come down directly from Ernest d'Amours, the State Attorney General, that a tight lid of secrecy should be placed over the entire investigation. With so much interest being paid to the crime he wanted no chance of embarrassing the state in front of the whole nation. Keller may have had little to say to the media but plenty of information about the probe made its way onto the front pages of the papers anyway.

Early interest was paid to the dates listed in Barbara's confession. Shortly after the arraignment a young couple came forward, first to the police and then to interviewers, to say that they believed they were the ones who had given Sylvester Roberts a ride home the night he was killed. The couple said they had picked a man up at the train station and then dropped him off at the now very well-known Gilmanton Iron Works farm. But they remembered that the date this happened was on the Sunday before Christmas, December 21. It was not a big discrepancy, only being a few days before the one that Barbara gave. But with a confession already secured the case was no whodunnit, even the smallest scraps of new information like this could raise a storm of interest. Enough uproar was raised by the couple's hitch-hiking story that William Keller double-checked the calendar. The Sunday before Christmas in 1946 had been the 22nd. So, it was found that the couple and Barbara were all incorrect. The couple had been off by one day. And while Barbara's confession mentioned several times the murder happened on a Sunday evening; it was just that she kept calling that Sunday the 23rd by honest mistake.

On September 23rd officials had to remove Barbara from Belknap County and take her to The New Hampshire State Hospital in Concord. William Keller had become increasingly concerned about her mental state and petitioned the court to allow him to have her evaluated. When the state hospital had been constructed in 1842 it was only the seventeenth mental institution to have been created in the entire country. It served the needs not just of the state's prisoners, like Barbara, but any New Hampshire resident impacted by mental illness. Different buildings catered to male and female patients, with elderly patients given a new state-of-the-art facility all their own.

Sheriff Crockett and Deputy Sheriff Fred Elliot drove Barbara to The New Hampshire State Hospital themselves just as soon as the judge granted permission. F. E. Normandin called it a routine two-week observation period but the truth was that Barbara had become increasingly agitated while confined to the county farm. Barbara was under an incredible strain and had no one but her oldest brother and her lawyer she could turn to. Her sister Marjorie did not seem capable, emotionally, of visiting her. Barbara was allowed no other visitors by order of the state. One unnamed woman from Alton, possibly her boyfriend's mother or one of her co-workers from the wool mill, had tried to visit her after her arraignment but had been turned away.

This did not mean however that Barbara was entirely cut off from the world. She met regularly with her brother

Charles during her consultations with F.E. Normandin. Charles brought her cigarettes and news of the rest of their family. Marjorie's son, born in the months before the confession, was getting bigger. Robert had picked up some side work at a mill. They did not discuss what was being printed about her in the newspapers.

Barbara also received a startling amount of mail by post. Fifty workers at the Scott & William Knitting Machine Mill where her brother-in-law Paul worked all wrote notes of encouragement and support in a card that they mailed to the girl during her confinement. Even though she had dropped out of school in the ninth grade many former schoolmates also sent her letters. Even the priest at the Federated Church in Gilmanton Iron Works, Reverend Dimock and his wife, wrote letters expressing their disappointment in not being able to visit Barbara in person. Rather than making pariahs of the Roberts family, the residents of Gilmanton rallied behind them. It was a tight-knit community and they had an enormous amount of sympathy and goodwill for the confessed killer. Many felt guilt that the abuses at the Roberts farm had continued on for so long without their being any the wiser.

Of course, there was fan mail: random letters from people Barbara had never met, and never would meet, but who had read her story in their own local papers and felt compelled to reach out to her. They came in from all corners of the country. The tone of most of these letters was supportive and sympathetic. A few came with marriage proposals, but only very few; another small percentage came with threats.

Two weeks exactly after dropping Barbara off at the state hospital in Concord Sheriff Crockett and Deputy Sheriff Elliot made the drive to the capitol once again. This time they picked up the prisoner and brought her back to Laconia. The doctors had declared that Barbara was sane and was healthy enough to stand trial.

Chapter Fifteen

Everything about Grace turned into a scandal. She had a knack for making people pay attention. — Laurie Wilkens

On October 28, 1947, the Grand Jury was convened with Judge William Grimes presiding. Judge Grimes, a native of Dover, New Hampshire, had been appointed to the bench only a few months earlier. At the age of thirty-six, he was the youngest Justice ever assigned to the New Hampshire Superior Court. He may have been new to the state's Superior Court but he was not new to law and justice. William Grimes had practiced law for the ten previous years, having graduated from the law school at Boston University in 1937. Still, it was a harsh start for the young Judge. There were seven cases going before the Grand Jury on that October morning: two of them were high profile and very carefully watched by the nation at large. Besides the Barbara Roberts case the court would also be hearing testimony and evidence against Evelyn Cote in the death of her toddler son. It would be a grim day of testimony for the jurors, and Judge Grimes, to hear.

With so many cases before the Grand Jury that day, witnesses for all seven cases lined the hallways, waiting for their turn to speak. It made it difficult for the press to tell who was there for which case. Reverend Frank P. Fletcher, from the Methodist Church in Meredith, led those who were waiting their turn in court in prayer. It was a long and exhausting day. A Meredith man pled not guilty to the attempted rape of a minor. Judge Grimes set his bail at $2,000 and sent him to be processed. Evelyn Cote also pled not guilty to manslaughter for the death of her son, and she also had bail set at $2,000. Charges were read against a husband and wife who were caught passing bad checks.

The Barbara Roberts case would not begin until 2:00 in the afternoon, after all the other matters going before the court that day were heard. The jury took a break for lunch at the Laconia Tavern before hearing the case against her. The tavern was housed in a historic hotel. Because of its location right near the courthouse, across from the Laconia library, it was a regular spot for lawyers, juries, and judges. In later years it would become known as a favorite hotspot for Grace Metalious and would put a new signature drink named 'Peyton Place,' Grace's favorite mix of Canadian Club whiskey and ginger ale with a light lemon twist, on the menu. In modern days the hotel where President Eisenhower once stayed is now subsidized housing.

The same witnesses that had testified at the earlier arraignment showed up again, Sheriff Crockett, Barbara's brother Charles, Dr. Gage, and State Trooper George McKeagney. New witnesses were also called to the stand: including her Uncle Charles and her boyfriend David. Barbara was not in court that day. She waited back at the Belknap County Farm anxiously waiting to get word from her lawyer as to the outcome. It would not be the news she hoped to hear.

Police had continued to refuse to accept the idea that the shapely young woman had been able to kill her father on her own and then also to drag his body through the back field to the family barn.

"I did this all alone,"[45] Barbara kept insisting throughout the investigation but people knew how she was when it came to her brother Billy. They believed she was just trying to shield the boy.

On October 28, 1947, the Grand Jury indicted William Roberts, along with his sister Barbara, for the second-degree murder of Sylvester Roberts. Despite Barbara's confession that she committed the crime on her own, there were inconsistencies with the story she had told. The investigation of the kitchen door and the bones of the victim found that two different guns had been used in the murder. Barbara had only said she did not know which of the two guns found in the house she had used to kill her father. Police couldn't understand how the girl could remember shooting Sylvester once but not that she had then picked up another weapon and shot him for a second time. Marjorie Roberts could not confirm that Billy had been Christmas shopping with her that evening. The police speculated that Billy had to have been the second shooter or, at the very least, had to have helped carry the dead weight of their father to the sheep pen for concealment.

The grand jury agreed with the police. On November 1, Barbara and Billy, for the first time together since Barbara's September confession, appeared before Judge Grimes to enter formal not guilty pleas. A series of charges were read against the two. Besides second-degree murder, each was charged with aiding and abetting the other when shooting their father and concealing his body beneath the sheep pen.

Spectators were not allowed in the courtroom but witnesses who were on hand to testify in another case being heard at the same time said the siblings were quiet and that Billy especially seemed nervous. Photographers for the area newspapers waited outside the doors to capture every possible image they could without being inside the courtroom. The stock photo of Barbara, eyes downcast, that the papers had been printing for the past two months was now replaced with a different kind of image. In this one she appeared younger, a smirk on her face, with a thin black bow at the collar of her white shirt and a beret tilted charmingly over her dark hair. She looks to her left, conspiratorially, towards her brother. Billy, with his slight build, looked like a much younger boy than he was. He was clad in a brown suit jacket and blue pants that were specially purchased or borrowed for his appearance in the court. The trial was set for December 1, 1947, after many months of waiting. Through it all the greatest champion of the two siblings would be their oldest brother, Charles.

"All we ask is for a chance to place the whole story before the jury and we are confident Barbara and Billy will be free,"[46] Charles said, speaking for the family, in a statement made in the days after it was publicly announced that a trial date had been set.

Charles and Robert had both dedicated themselves to staying in the area until the trial was complete. Tired of relying on their Uncle's hospitality after so many weeks of waiting the brothers had moved back into the Gilmanton Iron Works farmhouse where their father had been killed. Marjorie too, having no other option but to move in with her in-laws in Alton, was still living at the family home. Her husband Paul, whose family historically had been as tied to the sea as the Roberts family had been in England, had found that mill work was not for him. Returning to the Merchant Marines meant long weeks away from Marjorie and their son but it also meant a reprieve from the notoriety that came with being attached to his wife's family. Marjorie's husband had left but having her older brothers there to help around the farm was some small consolation.

For the first time in many months Barbara and Billy also would, in a way, be sharing a living situation also. In a surprise move the court sent Billy to the Belknap County Farm instead of to the State Industrial School for the four weeks until the trial would begin. This was not to be a true reunion for the pair though. Superintendent Flanders had been given strict orders to keep the siblings separate— the two could not talk to or see each other at all over the course of the month. Both were, more or less, confined to their rooms in a more prison-like way than Barbara had faced previously. Superintendent Flanders brought them both outside to walk the property several times a day, but they were always brought out separately and at different times. He would tell reporters they were in good spirits.

Chapter Sixteen

She set out to lift the lid off a small New England town and wound up pulling it off its hinges.
— Hal Boyle, writing about Grace Metalious

After so many months of anticipation the trial got off to a lackluster start. Barbara and Billy were brought to the courthouse shortly before jury selection was set to begin at 10:00. The Attorneys Normandin had been instructed to have their clients brought to the side entrance on Academy Street. There was a lot of worry among the officers of the court about how many spectators and press might be found at the front entrance. Sheriff Crockett was charged with picking the siblings up at the Belknap County Farm and getting them to court on time. In the end all the concerns about an unruly mob were a storm in a teacup. Only a very small number of spectators showed up and not nearly as many members of the press as had been predicted. The veteran news reporters knew that little of interest would happen on the first day.

While the court was called to order at 10:00 a.m. lawyers from both sides gathered around the bench with Judge William Grimes for a conference. At times the conversation at the bench grew animated but no one could hear a word of what was said.

It was not until noon that day that the jury selection actually began. The jury was quickly chosen along with an unusual number of alternates, nearly doubling the size of the panel usually seen at trials. This jury of the Roberts' peers were all men. At this point only one woman, Harriet Richardson of Dover, had ever served on a jury in the state of New Hampshire and that had occurred just the past September. The Normandin lawyers were representing both Billy and Barbara, as their cases were being tried together. The prosecutor in the case would be the Attorney General, Ernest R. d'Amours, assisted by County Solicitor William Keller. After giving the jury their instructions Judge Grimes sent them home for the evening, anticipating that a lengthy court case would ensue first thing beginning the next day.

Daniel Richardson, who worked for a grocery wholesaler was named foreman. Other jurors selected included: George W. Talson, William Nelson, George F. Hughes, Richard Lancaster, Herbert L. Mansfield, Howard W. Bailey, Van Ness Choate, Martin Bernard, Harry Wallace, Frank W. Abbott, and Ashley Mason. Lazarus Valliere was chosen as the principal alternate juror in case any of them fell ill. Then William Sister, John Hoey, Charles H. Lyman, George Wells, Frank DeHaven Jr., Peter Landry, Charles Shortie, Charles Simpson, William Nelson, Raymond Willett, and Charles J. Goss, were all named extra alternates, probably because there was a belief that the trial would go on for some time. The fate of Barbara Roberts, who was now twenty-one years old, and her seventeen-year-old brother Billy were in their hands.

The trial took place at the Belknap County Courthouse at 64 Court Street in Laconia, New Hampshire. The court was a large deep red brick building, built in 1893. It had a series of arches along one side, and a tower that rose several stories higher than the rest of the two-story structure. Its sharply steepled hip roof made the building look larger than it really was, and far, far more imposing. It could probably have been mistaken for a church if there was not already a fine white example of that kind of building located directly across the street.

In the 1970s an extension would be added to the historic building, with panes of glass as seen in a modern office building hidden behind four brick arches to keep the new addition in line with the style of the older part of the structure. Today it is no longer used as a courthouse but serves as the offices for Belknap County.

Chapter Seventeen

I know too much about New England villages.
I'd much rather they were beautiful.
— Grace Metalious, quoted in "The Girl from 'Peyton Place'"

The next day the second-degree murder trial began in earnest. First up was a reading of the full charges against the accused. The words "feloniously, willfully, and with malice aforethought"47 were repeated several times. Barbara, who was required to stand during the reading of the charges against her, managed to keep the calm demeanor she had become known for. Then the entire court left on a field trip of sorts. Judge Grimes, the members of the jury, and the assorted lawyers were loaded into a bright yellow school bus. They were all going to take a trip to the Roberts' Farm to see the scene of the killing for themselves. It would be the first time Barbara had been back to her childhood home since before giving her confession on that unseasonably hot September evening.

Billy Roberts had asked, and was given permission, to stay at the Belknap County Farm under the supervision of Superintendent Flanders and his wife while everyone else viewed the house. But at the last possible moment the teenaged prisoner changed his mind and asked to go. He and Barbara were driven to the Gilmanton Iron Works farmhouse in a red sedan, the personal vehicle of Sheriff

Crockett. Their sister Marjorie and brother Charles were home to greet the jury when they arrived. Marjorie's two black dogs, one small and one large, barked incessantly as the school bus transporting all of the jurors, Judge Grimes, and the handful of reporters and photographers who had been invited to come on the trip, came up the driveway.

Billy, for reasons of his own, refused to leave the car once at the farm. But during the hour the jurors spent at the house Barbara got to have a reunion of sorts with her sister and brother. Deputy Sheriff Chester Bickford, who doubled as the Meredith Fire Chief, stayed behind to watch over the accused. Barbara was dressed in the black suit and bow tie, prim and proper gloves on her hands, that had already come to be known as something of her court uniform. She sat in the large family room at the center of the house, which was dominated on opposite ends by dueling fireplaces. She got to play with her nephew, Marjorie's son David, for the first time. The boy was nearly a year old, but Barbara had only seen him a few times as a newborn before she had been sent to jail. Her brother-in-law Paul had recently returned home on furlough from the Merchant Marines, and he idled around the farm making small repairs while the jurors were given the tour of the property. The only family members missing were Robert, who was working the early shift at the mill, and Billy who decided to stay in the car.

The barn where Sylvester's body had lain hidden for nine months was still standing, though Paul had recently put a jaunty red roof on the old building with help from his brothers-in-law. The barn was filled with hay, but it housed no livestock. With Paul away at sea most of the time and Marjorie chasing an energetic toddler around, it was thought animals would be more trouble than they were worth once the trial was ended, and Charles and Robert left. There were several holes in the floor of the barn and the attached sheep pen. Jurors were encouraged to shine flashlights around and to climb inside them. They were told they would hear interesting testimony about the holes the next day.

Next the large pool of jurors and alternates were brought to see the inside of the farmhouse. William Keller pointed out some holes in the wall where bullets had been found and explained that the kitchen door they were seeing that day was a replacement for the one he had sent to the State Trooper headquarters back in September.

On display throughout the house were the dress uniforms and formal caps of the Roberts and Richards families. Art prints of ships and other ocean scenes were hung neatly on the walls. Here and there framed tapestries, which looked as if they had been brought back from the distant ports the men visited while at sea, were hung throughout the home. Marjorie wore a black dress and seemed nervous. She did not seem to know how to respond to the large group of strangers walking through her house.

Charles Roberts showed the crowd the cellar and told them the history of the house, he believed the original colonial it had grown from dated back to the early 1700s. During his time at home waiting for the trial to begin he had made some improvements to the property, assisting Paul in putting the new roof on the barn and replacing the part of the kitchen wall the police had taken when they removed the door. F.A Normandin explained to jurors what furniture was new since the night of the murder and described how the layout of the house had differed slightly on that fateful night.

All in all there was a casual, almost party, atmosphere to the trip. Snow had not yet begun to fall that season and it was warmer than it normally was in December in New Hampshire. Jurors posed in different spots around the farm for the photographer's cameras. They gathered for several large group shots in front of the farmhouse. Marjorie came out, a white apron tied over her black dress, with her son David in her arms. When the child began to fuss at being held captive by his mother the photographers handed him the burnt-out flashbulbs from their cameras. He tapped them together happily, seemingly amused by the sound they made.

The makeshift musical instruments didn't hold the child's attention for long. He dropped them to the ground and started to eye one of the reporters. Katherine Donovon, probably the best-known female reporter in Boston (she covered news for the *Boston Record*, a paper that would later merge several times and become *The Boston Herald*), was wearing a brightly colored suit that seemed to attract the little boy's gaze. David reached for her and Marjorie passed him over to the reporter. Katherine Donovon happily bounced him on her hip for a few minutes. Noticing that Marjorie's eyes had begun to fill with tears she handed the baby back to her.

Chapter Eighteen

That was where the shoe pinched. You get angrier about the truth than you do about lies.
— Grace Metalious, to the St. Louis Post-Dispatch

The next morning the trial began in much the same way as the previous day. Attorney General d'Amours, William Keller, and the Attorneys Normandin gathered together in conversation around the bench with Judge Grimes. The jurors, expecting more of the same, settled in for the wait.

After some brief back and forth the judge rose from his seat and mentioned for the lawyers to follow him. Barbara and Billy remained in the courtroom, sitting patiently in their seats, with Robert and Charles sitting on either side of them. It was not until around four that afternoon that a bailiff entered the room and asked the accused to follow him, Charles and Robert leaping up to follow.

Behind the scenes, away from the eyes of the jurors, a conference was being held. After speaking to Billy and Barbara together the two were separated and consulted again in private. Within twenty minutes Judge Grimes was once again seated in the courtroom, rapping his gavel loudly on the podium to silence the curious murmurings coming from the jurors and spectators. In the sudden quiet a clerk spoke out. He asked Barbara if she wanted to change her plea. She told him that she did.

"Guilty to manslaughter in the first degree."[48] She called out in a calm, clear voice and sat down while Billy rose to repeat the same words.

The clerk wrote hastily on a piece of paper and handed it to Judge Grimes, who signed his name to it before passing it to the Attorney General.

"After very careful weighing of all factors in this case, counsel for the state is prepared to recommend and does recommend a sentence of three to five years in the State Prison for Barbara Roberts and a continuation of sentence and probation for four years with a letter of instruction from the court, in the case of William,"[49] d'Amours announced to the shocked courtroom

It was a surprise to many as both Attorneys Normandin had spoken convincingly for months of their belief that the siblings would walk free from the courthouse come the end of the trial. Barbara, it was later announced, had wanted to plead guilty from the start but refused to until she was promised that Billy would not be sent to a state institution. She felt compelled to fulfill the promise that she had made to her mother to watch out for the boy. Every decision she made, was made with the reverent hope that "everything will be alright with him."[50] By the same token, taking the plea deal also spared Billy and Marjorie from having to testify to the abuse they had witnessed and received over the years.

As quickly as that the trial was over, and the court adjourned. It was an unexpected, and for some, a disappointing ending to the trial that had for a time promised to be one for the ages— at least in a relatively low crime state like New Hampshire.

Charles, who had attended to his brother and sister closely throughout the ordeal and who had always supported them when talking to the press, reiterated that they believed the pair would have been found not guilty at the end of a trial. He credited the pair's "strong sense of justice"[51] for their decision to plead guilty when so many had been convinced they'd be set free. Barbara in particular, Charles said, "wanted to face the penalty"[52] for shooting her father, no matter what reasons she had for doing so. During the negotiations she had even offered to serve more time than what was being suggested as punishment for the crime.

The letter of instruction that had been mentioned during the sentencing for William Roberts stipulated that he be "placed in a suitable institution until otherwise ordered by the court."[53] Soon after it was announced that he would serve his probation in state custody at The Golden Rule Farm, in Tilton New Hampshire. It was expected that when Barbara became eligible for parole, she would petition the court to take custody of him.

From the start it was well-publicized that Barbara would not serve a full three to five years in prison. State law mandated that parole could be considered after she served a third of her sentence and she would be credited up to three days a month off her sentence for good behavior. Chances were good that she would free long before three years came up.

County Solicitor William Keller, in an apparent nod to the abuse suffered by the Roberts children at the hands of their father, told the reporters that there were strong circumstances that had prompted the state to agree to reduce the charges in exchange for a guilty plea.

Barbara Roberts said she hoped that while she was in prison, she could start up the education that had been ended so prematurely in the ninth grade. She added, briefly, before being led away, "I'm looking forward to the day when I can get out and come home to keep house once again for my brothers."[54]

"She and Billy must have suffered terribly while I was away," Charles said, speaking to the press gathered on the courthouse steps for the final time. "We all suffered."[55]

Chapter Nineteen

Grace wrote what people were thinking.
She had the courage to write about those
things nobody else would write about.
— Laurie Wilkins

The "suitable institution" for Billy Robert was The Golden Rule Farm, in Tilton New Hampshire. This was a private facility, in accordance with the promise to Barbara that he would not go to a state institution. The organization had a good reputation and was often referred to as "New England's own Boys town."56 Originally envisioned as an orphanage, housed in the former home of the sister of New Hampshire statesman Daniel Webster, over time it had evolved into an alternate setting for minors who would otherwise be sent to an adult prison. Like the Belknap County Farm of the State Industrial School, its scope had changed slightly over the years to offer more opportunities for rehabilitation and less for punishment.

Billy's experience at The Golden Rule Farm probably was similar to the one his sister had faced at the Belknap County Farm. During the time Billy spent there the Golden Rule Farm could be considered home to as many as fifty boys between the ages of eight and eighteen. An article written in 1940 about the farm painted an idyllic picture of what life was like there for these boys. It described the farm as "large and well-stocked,"[57] and a "haven for the treatment of underprivileged boys who have the possibilities of becoming useful citizens."[58] The farm, the article went on, was overrun with "a more courteous unspoiled group of boys as you'd ever meet."[59] This was juxtaposed with a much grimmer picture of the lives these future useful citizens had left behind:

> Life before it brought them to the farm is best forgotten. Most of them were wretched, lonely, and unwanted. From babyhood they were soon taught that there was no place in the world for them. They were born to poverty or undesirable environments and unless something intervened, they could expect nothing else. They never knew the contentment of a normal comfortable home.[60]

As at the poor farm that Barbara had been housed in for the past few months, the boys at Golden Rule Farm were put to work, given jobs that were suited to their health, their age, and their temperament. Some raised livestock. Others farmed the land. But Golden Rule Farm tried to create a warmer and more enriching home for its wards than the poorhouses normally did for their residents. All of the boys were expected to go to school. They were welcome to invite friends over to play and parties were held annually that everyone in town could attend. Many of the boys took part in after-school sports and others would go to the games to cheer them on. Some of the boys even showed up at the farm with their dogs from home trailing behind them. Even though pets were not expressly allowed, most of the time they were not turned away.

The farm was made up of a large white two-story farmhouse and several smaller cottages which featured house mothers and/or fathers to watch over the boys that were living in them. While Billy was no doubt homesick for the sister who was more like a mother to him, Golden Rule Farm must have also seemed like a respite after his hard life in Gilmanton Iron Works and the whirlwind of the past year. The press was not allowed to hound him and the officials in charge of the establishment declined to give public updates on how or what he was doing.

Chapter Twenty

Everybody knew that the South was degenerate. Grace Metalious' books insist— usually stridently— that Puritan New England has all the Southern vices and a few others that not even William Faulkner had come across.
— Merle Miller, Ladies Home Journal

Barbara faced a much different kind of life after the conclusion of the murder trial. The same evening that the state accepted her guilty plea she found herself, once again, in Sheriff Homer Crockett's red sedan, with the High Sheriff and Deputy Sheriff Fred Elliott. They took her to the state prison in Concord, but this was not the place where she would serve out her sentence. The next morning, on December 6th, she was transferred to Vermont's Riverside Women's Reformatory in Rutland.

From the 1880s until the early 1940s New Hampshire had allowed its female prisoners to be incarcerated in the South Wing of the state prison located in Concord. But, in all those years, the state never had more than six women prisoners incarcerated at one time. It was not seen as economical to keep an entire wing set aside, and to maintain the hire of the female chaperones that were needed to ensure the safety of the female prisoners, for such a small number of ladies. Beginning in 1941 New Hampshire made arrangements to send any female inmates in state custody to the Riverside Women's Reformatory in Rutland, Vermont.

It was when Barbara was transported to Rutland early the next morning after her trial that the stress of the past year caught up to her, much as it had in her first few days at the Belknap County Farm. She was in Vermont only a few hours before she collapsed in her room and a doctor was called to come check on her health.

"The ordeal which the poor girl had to undergo was too much for her," the press was informed by the Superintendent of the prison, Helen Koltonski. "We all feel very sorry for her."[61]

In Rutland, Barbara found she was not as notable as she had felt for the past year in New Hampshire with all of the media attention that was paid to her case. Other Riverside Women's Reformatory inmates during her incarceration included Ethel May Curtis, who the F.B.I named the foremost female bogus check artist in the country. Curtis had warrants in 26 states when she was arrested for passing a fake $1,034 check in Concord, New Hampshire. When she was caught, state and Federal agents found identification for more than forty different aliases on her person. The state sentenced her to five to seven years, to be served in Rutland. Ethel May had already escaped once from the prison by the time Barbara arrived.

Even with some of these more career prisoners that graced its hallways being sent to the Riverside Reformatory, the place was considered an easy place to serve out one's sentence. Even at its peak occupation the entire building never housed more than fifty prisoners at any given time. When Barbara was transferred there she was one of just eighteen prisoners. While many of those sent from other states were considered hardened criminals, the majority of the inmates were really there because of "crimes against morality" or "crimes against chastity." This was a polite way of saying they were adulterers or prostitutes.

Riverside may not have been the Belknap County Farm, but it was not a high-security building surrounded by barbed wire or men with guns. For one, the unemployment offices for the state of Vermont were housed inside the prison. This shows that, overall, the women prisoners kept there were not seen as dangerous or in need of strict segregation from the rest of the world. Over the course of the prison's history different women's organizations, priests, a 4-H club, and even the Rotary would all use the reformatory communal areas to hold meetings and events. This was not the prison most people imagine when they think of someone serving time for a murder conviction— or even first-degree manslaughter.

As before the trial, Barbara was not allowed visitors during her time at Riverside, a decision that was made by New Hampshire prison warden Charles Clark. And it was the New Hampshire warden who had jurisdiction over her even if she was being housed in a Vermont prison. It snowed on Barbara's first day there and after her fainting spell she did what she had always done. She went to work. Her first task was shoveling the freshly fallen snow off the prison yard. Long term she worked seven hours a day sewing in the prison laundry room.

The reformatory building had been used as a men's prison from 1876 to 1919. It should have been a bleak and forbidding place. But when Barbara Roberts arrived in Vermont the interior of the building had been painted a sunshiny yellow, with delicate curtains at every window. The prison arranged outings to nearby Lake Bomoseen for prisoners to take day trips or would take them to see the latest Hollywood movies in the Rutland theaters. Instead of guards, the women were watched over by female matrons, who acted more like sorority house mothers for each block than they did prison officers. The women prisoners did laundry for many businesses and families in town, they were charged with tending to a large garden each spring and summer and were known affectionately for the candy apples they handed out to Rutland's Trick-or-Treating children every Halloween.

The unusual situation at Riverside can be credited back to Lena Ross, who spent twenty-five years as a first-grade teacher before being appointed the first Superintendent of the Riverside Women's Reformatory. People would say that as a teacher she had seen firsthand some of the conditions that prisoners had grown up in and that it gave her the sympathy needed to try to treat them differently. It was Ross who originally scraped the blackout gray paint from the many windows in the building, knocked down walls to create wide-open common spaces, and began many of the community outreach programs for prisoners. Lena Ross was a firm believer that "healthy pride, workmanlike responsibility and social solidarity"[62] were what her charges were most in need of— not locked doors and weapon-wielding guards.

By the time Barbara arrived at Riverside Lena Ross was long retired but the prisoners were still often called "Miss Lena's girls" by Rutland residents. Her ideas on how a prison should be run were continued under the watchful eye of the new Superintendent, Helen Koltonski, who had worked under her for many years before taking over the position. There was, after all, no reason to change something that was working so well. Since the start of the Riverside Reformatory less than 6% of its prisoners would ever be incarcerated again for a repeat offense and, Ethyl May Curtis being the exception and not the rule, there had only ever been three escape attempts. This even though there were no locked doors or prison guards. While Barbara was incarcerated, she was surrounded by art, with original paintings depicting children and mothers hung on the walls, and the windows were open wide behind the cheery curtains to let in fresh air.

Luck, and most likely the popular public opinion of her, was truly was on Barbara's side when she was sent to Vermont and not to one of the other women's institutions in

New England. Most of which were seen as much rougher and not as humane as what she faced in Vermont. However, that is also judging them by the standards of their time. A year after Barbara started her sentence in Vermont the women's prison in Framingham, Massachusetts was engulfed in scandal. Dr. Marriam Van Waters, the Framingham warden, was not only fired but was also brought up on criminal charges because she ignored a "sex racket" going on in the women's prison she was in charge of. Later court records reveal that what was meant by "sex racket" was really "crushes, courtships, and homosexual practices among the inmates at the reformatory."[63] In the 1940s criminality amongst the female population was accepted, if not expected, but homosexuality was a bridge too far.

New Hampshire continued to send its female inmates to Vermont and to the Massachusetts Correctional Institution in Framingham through the 1980s. Conditions in the out-of-state facilities were not always adequate for the female prisoners. As mindsets began to change about prisons it was thought that sending women far away from their families during their sentences led to them having fewer ties with their communities, which could lead to recidivism and future jail sentences that were costly to taxpayers. In the 1980s a group of women prisoners sued New Hampshire and won. The courts decreed that the state needed to create its own facilities for its women prisoners and stop sending them out of state.

Initially New Hampshire used older, smaller buildings that had once been used for men to house their female prisoners. It would not be until 2013 that the state would put aside money to construct a brand new facility in Concord designed specifically for its women inmates.

Chapter Twenty-One

To a tourist these towns look as peaceful as a postcard picture. But if you go beneath that picture, it's like turning over a rock with your foot- all kinds of strange things crawl out. Everybody who lives in town knows what's going on- there are no secrets- but they don't want outsiders to know.
– Grace Metalious, in an interview with Hal Boyle

Barbara Roberts killing of her father will sound familiar to anyone who's read *Peyton Place*. The novel is split into three separate parts. The first section starts in 1937 and introduces the reader to a number of residents of the small New Hampshire town of Peyton Place. Much of the book is centered on the unusual friendship between Selena Cross and Allison MacKenzie. They are an unlikely duo. Selena Cross, smart and beautiful, comes from the wrong side of the tracks. Her mother, Nellie, works as a housekeeper in the MacKenzie household. Allison MacKenzie is the book smart daughter of a widow named Constance who owns a dress shop in town. Both girls have difficult relationships with their parents. Allison can never understand why her mother becomes upset when she asks questions about her father, whom she is told had passed away when she was a baby. Selena is tasked with caring for a younger brother while dealing with abuse and sexual advances from her stepfather Lucas. Woven throughout the two girl's stories we see firsthand the abuses that the segregated social stratification in town produces. Rich mill owners, and their sons, are able to get away with all kinds of unruly behavior while the lower classes are held to a much higher moral standard, their every decision picked apart and second-guessed by the types of people Grace Metalious had fought against her entire life.

Part Two starts up two years later. Constance MacKenzie has begun an increasingly passionate love affair with the sultry new school principal in town, Tom Makris. In a fit of anger, she confesses to Allison the truth about her father—Constance was not a widow, that was a story she had crafted after finding herself pregnant by a man who was already married to someone else. Constance had returned to Peyton Place when Allison was still a baby and altered the date on her birth certificate to save herself and her child from the shame of illegitimacy. Selena Cross too is forced to come to terms with the harsh truth about her own parents. Selena finds herself pregnant, unwillingly, at the hands of her stepfather. It's a situation that drives her mother to suicide instead of coming to her daughter's aid. Rather, the only help comes at the hands of the local medical man, Doctor Swain, who performs an illegal abortion. Dr. Swain confronts Lucas with what he knows and chases him out of town.

Part Three takes another leap forward, three years this time. Allison had graduated from high school and won a few small awards for her short stories. She is looking to escape Peyton Place and the increasingly strained relationship with her mother, who has settled into wedded bliss with Tom Makris, so she uses her talent at writing to propel her all the way to New York City. There she falls into the same pattern her mother had in the city years earlier, involved in a sordid affair with a married man who promises to propel her career.

Selena Cross has become an integral part of Constance's dress shop. Despite the poverty she was raised in the town thinks well of her, she is levelheaded and hard working. But then her stepfather Lucas reappears at their farmhouse one evening. Selena kills him and in desperation hides his body beneath the floorboards of the farm's sheep pen. In time the murder is discovered, and Peyton Place is shocked when Selena is arrested for the crime. During the eagerly anticipated trial, Dr. Swain reveals the terrible abuse Selena suffered at the hands of her stepfather and admits to having performed an abortion to save the girl from having to live with the consequences of Lucas' crimes against her. Selena is acquitted, thanks to the truth about her plight being brought to light.

We don't know for sure how much of the novel Grace had crafted before Laurie Wilkens shared the story of Barbara Roberts with her. In later interviews Grace would insist that the novel was "three-fourths written before I ever moved to Gilmanton."[64] But by that point Grace was also tired of defending her novel and trying to convince her neighbors it was a work of fiction and not about them. It is clear just from reading the manuscript in its published form that learning the fate of Sylvester and his daughter was a huge catalyst in the creation of the story.

Grace had spent much of the start of her time in Gilmanton working on a novel she called *The Quiet Place*, which centered around the struggles of a young married couple while the husband attends college after serving time in the military. Grace would pick the name Jacques Chambrun out of a list of agents she found at the town library, later admitting she went to him first because of the French name. She mailed Chambrun a five-page long letter and 312 pages of *The Quiet Place*. While *The Quiet Place* would never be published, it was rejected by six publishers before Grace gave up on it, it was a strong enough first attempt that it was able to land Grace the kind of New York agent she was convinced she needed to sell her work. Later she would learn that Chambrun had a terrible reputation because he had stolen funds from many of the authors he represented. Many questioned if the agent was even French at all and believed he hailed from the Bronx though he spoke the language fluently enough when he needed to.

On August 17, 1955, the well at "It'll Do" had been dry for nine weeks straight. Grace and the kids carried empty milk cartons four miles round trip to a nearby spring to get drinking water. Grace fed the kids lettuce and tomato sandwiches for lunch before bringing them to the town park for a swim since they had no running water for a bath. She came home, the kids tired and sandy after a day playing at the beach, to find that her entire life had just been upended. After five rejections of *Peyton Place* (originally submitted under the name *The Tree and the Blossom*, an allusion to the book's focus on parents and children) Grace, much like Barbara Roberts more than a decade before her, found that a telegram was waiting for her. And, just like Barbara, Grace did not even need to read it to know what it contained, though hers was much more eagerly awaited news.

"Gee-Gee, come quick, hurry!" she yelled to George. "He's sold it!"[65]

A quick call to Jacques Chambrun confirmed the news. Julian Messner Inc had bought *The Tree and the Blossom.* Grace was so excited she did not even think to ask how much the novel had sold for.

Grace's next call would be to her neighbor Laurie Wilkins. Remembering the day years later Laurie would say of Grace that she "would never be really poor or really happy again."[66]

Chapter Twenty-Two

Run for your life, there's trouble coming.
— Grace Metalious

Given the racy nature of *Peyton Place,* and the utter lack of publishing credits to the author's name, it is not surprising that several publishers passed it by before it found its way to a boutique publisher called Julian Messner, Inc. Julian Messner was one of only two major New York publishers of the day run by a woman. Long before the feminist revolution of the 1960s Kitty Messner was a force of female independence and empowerment. She wore expensive bespoke pantsuits that she had carefully patterned after men's business wear. The eponymous publishing firm she took over after the death of her husband Julian was staffed almost entirely by women— not just the secretaries and typists, but the editors, the sales directors, the manuscript readers, and publicists. It was the rare company where women were in the majority. Where other large publishers had looked at *Peyton Place* and seen only scandal Kitty Messner looked at it and saw something more.

That's not to say Julian Messner Inc accepted the manuscript exactly as it was and had no concerns about the content. Minor lines, mostly sexual in nature, were rewritten or cut entirely. A few inconsequential secondary characters were also removed for bogging down the story instead of moving it along. Then came the biggest edit of them all, the hardest one to stomach in Grace's eyes. While the publisher thought they could handle a novel with pre-marital sex, masturbation, illegitimate children, rape, and abortion, Kitty Messner worried that an incestuous relationship between a father and daughter would be the final straw for the readers of the 1950s. Lucas Cross, the character Grace Metalious had based on Sylvester Roberts however loosely, was quickly edited out as Selena's father. In the published edition he was called her stepfather, a small concession to the delicacies of the readers. This was also the only editorial change that Grace fought. She would later lament to Laurie Wilkins that the change "ruined my book, now it's trash rather than tragedy."[67] It was not that Grace felt any real responsibility to stick closely to the story of Barbara Roberts and Sylvester. The author worried that it would not seem realistic that a doctor would perform an illegal abortion if there was not the specter of a child born with genetic or medical malformations due to the close relationship between its parents.

It's funny to think that in the end the most shocking part of the "book everyone was talking about" was also the part that cut most undeniably to the truth. While people would cluck their tongues over the dirty mind of that Gilmanton housewife, it was the things she made up herself that were the ones that were considered sanitized enough to be published. Grace would later tell confidants like Bob Athearn that, after the editing process, *Peyton Place* had ended up not at all like the book she had set out to write.

When Kitty Messner bought the book, she envisioned a small run and hopefully some modest sales. The person who really saw something bigger in the future for the book was a Julian Messner Inc editor by the name of Howard Goodkind. He convinced Kitty to increase the advertising budget for the book and then hired a press agent from outside the company who had never promoted a novel before.

The PR man, Bud Brandt, used some of the advertising budget to travel out to Gilmanton to meet Grace Metalious for himself. Bud Brandt didn't know exactly what it was that he was looking for but he figured he could find a hook to market the book on if he looked long enough. It would be an understatement to say that Grace came as a surprise to Brandt. Even when dealing with her publisher she stuck to the same denim jeans and men's shirt, her hair carelessly thrown back in a ponytail, as she wore around the house. Deciding that Grace was unchangeable Brandt embraced this image. He had originally envisioned an author photo of a wholesome housewife in a dress and pearls. But after meeting Grace in person, he knew his original idea would never work. The most famous image of Grace shows her in her usual uniform, hunched over a Remington typewriter with her feet up on the desk. Larry Smith, a colleague of Laurie Wilkens at the *Laconia Evening Citizen*, took this picture which would become known as "Pandora in blue jeans." This was the image that would be printed as the author photo for *Peyton Place*.

In the end it wasn't the "ripped from the headlines" aspect of *Peyton Place* or even the unique character of its author that brought so much attention to the book's release. It was the animosity Gilmanton felt for Grace Metalious that did it. That first weekend in New Hampshire, Grace took Brandt on a tour of Gilmanton, telling little anecdotes about her neighbors and having him visit a Grange supper. It was while on this New Hampshire visit that Grace made an offhand comment that *Peyton Place* would probably lose George his school principal job. Like many of Grace's inventions it was true . . . but only sort of. Many Gilmanton residents had opposed George's hiring as the principal at the Gilmanton Corners School from the start. His ethnicity had been raised as a mark against him when he was hired a year previously and, while the rumors about his wife's book certainly were taken as a judgment against him, it was only one of several issues raised by residents. While George had been hired despite the opposition it had only come about thanks to the intervention of a lawyer and the contract had been stipulated for only one year. The town of Gilmanton would maintain that it was not so much that George was fired as they simply chose not to renew his contract when it expired. But in the end, it didn't matter what the town said. Grace's version of the truth won, as it usually did. Even more importantly, for the marketing of *Peyton Place*, the hook was found.

Within a few days, newspapers across the country, many of the same ones that ten years before had trumpeted the escapades of Barbara Roberts as the Lady-Like Killer, now featured headlines about the forthcoming book that was so outrageous that the author's husband had been fired for it. During a time when the average first novel by an unknown author could expect to sell two thousand copies total, *Peyton Place* sold sixty thousand copies in the first ten days of its release. The demand was so high that Julian Messner Inc had to ration copies of it when it came time to distribute, just to make sure that bookstores all around the country could get at least a few copies. Two weeks after the book's release 20th Century Fox negotiated the movie rights, earning Grace another $125,000 on top of the book royalties. After the movie came out, the book outsold *Gone with the Wind.* Within six months the book set publishing records: it was the fastest-selling novel in the history of publishing, and it was the best-selling first book of all time. One year after that the book achieved an even greater milestone— *Peyton Place* was the best-selling novel ever published up to that time.

All this happened despite some very large obstacles to sales. Many places would flat out just not carry the book. It was illegal to even mail a copy to anyone in Australia, Canada, South Africa, or the Soviet Union. One library in Beverly Farms, Massachusetts put a large sign out on their front lawn that read "This library does not carry *Peyton Place*. If you want it, go to Salem." A Providence, Rhode Island bookseller faced fines and imprisonment when he was accused of selling it to a minor. If Gilmanton residents wanted a copy, they had to drive to nearby Laconia to get it; there was not one single retailer in town that would carry the book. A bookstore in nearby Meredith, New Hampshire graced their window with a sign reading "*Peyton Place* is here— I don't know why you want to read it, but we are selling it for $3.95." A Laconia bookshop reported selling hundreds of copies.

Grace wanted to use her *Peyton Place* money to leave "It'll Do"— with its dodgy well and the windows that sometimes fell straight out of their frames— behind like a bad dream and to buy a real home. There was a house in Gilmanton on Meadow Pond Road that had long been a dream of hers— one she never could have guessed would someday come true. She and George used to picnic behind the house, sometimes even breaking in and eating their lunch inside. It was a 180-year-old Cape Cod, white, and it rambled in that kind of pleasing way that many old New England houses have about them. Thrilling Grace even more— the house had a notorious reputation. The house had stood alone at the far end of a small twisty dirt road, fully furnished but abandoned for many years due to its connection with a murderer that pre-dated that of Sylvester Roberts by many years.

Herman Mudgett was born in Gilmanton in 1861. He is better known today as H.H. Holmes, and under that name is considered by many to be America's first serial killer. From an early age he expressed an interest in medicine, though this took the form of seeing how long he could perform surgery on animals before they died. Young Mudgett grew up looking at Nahum Wight as a mentor of sorts. Dr. Wight was a Gilmanton doctor who found nationwide fame as an advocate for human dissection. At the age of sixteen,

Herman Mudgett married a Gilmanton girl by the name of Clara Lovering and soon fathered a child. The young family moved with him while he pursued his degree. Mudgett put himself through medical school, and supported his wife and son, by stealing cadavers and using them to defraud insurance companies in a series of scams.

Dr. Mudgett became Dr. Holmes as a matter of necessity. He killed a patient in Philadelphia, either accidentally or purposefully, and needed a fresh start. Clara, tired of his abuse and increasingly dark behavior, took their son and fled back to New Hampshire. She took refuge in her family home and would not see her husband again for many years.

Dr. Holmes appeared in Chicago just in time to take advantage of the wild influx of visitors coming to the Windy City for the World's Columbian Exposition, better known as the World's Fair. Dr. Holmes bought a pharmacy on credit and killed the woman he bought it from when she threatened to take him to court for non-payment. On 63rd Street, across the street from the pharmacy, Dr. Holmes built a remarkable three-story building that took up an entire city block. Dubbed "The Castle" by Chicagoans it featured shops at the street level and a rabbit's warren of booby-trapped rooms, said to number in the hundreds, above. Inside doors opened to nothing, stairs led to bricked over walls, and some rooms featured hidden gas pipes that could be turned on with the flip of a switch to kill the occupants while they slept. Riddled with secret passageways the building, named The World's Fair Hotel by Dr. Holmes, featured a greased shaft that could be used to send dead bodies directly to the basement where a surgical table, a vat of acid, and an eight-foot-long oven that could fit a fully grown man waited for them.

An estimated 27.5 million visitors would walk the canal-lined fairway of the Great White City created for the World's Fair. At least thirty-six, and maybe as many as two hundred of them, would lose their lives to Dr. Holmes. We know that Dr. Holmes visited the fair at least twice himself, accompanied by two sisters who would fall victim to the serial killer after enjoying the spectacle of the fair.

Along the way, Dr. Holmes also married three women, though he never divorced his first wife, who was still patiently back home in New Hampshire raising their son. Many of the wives, and the estimated one hundred and fifty stenographers and secretaries he employed over his years in Chicago, signed over property and money they had to Dr. Holmes. Many were never heard from again.

Ultimately, it wasn't murder, polygamy or even missing secretaries that knocked over the first domino towards taking down Dr. Holmes. It was simple insurance fraud. With an insurance investigator hot on his trail, Dr. Holmes began a bizarre state-crossing adventure that included a stop back to his boyhood home in Gilmanton to visit his wife and son.

With surprisingly little fanfare the Boston Police were able to arrest Dr. Holmes just before he could flee to Europe. In custody he confessed to, and then retracted, any number of murders and cons. Some of the people he said he killed later turned up very much alive. Some of the people he was known to have killed he refused to take credit for.

"I was born with the devil in me," Holmes would write in one of his many confessions. "I could not help the fact that I was a murderer, no more than the poet can help the inspiration to sing—I was born with the 'Evil One' standing as my sponsor beside the bed where I was ushered into the world, and he has been with me since."[68]

On May 7, 1896, Dr. Holmes was led to the gallows and hanged until he was dead. It was nine days short of his thirty-fifth birthday. With his last words, he offered one final retraction of all of his previous confessions. As the hangman's noose swung in front of him, Holmes claimed to have killed just two women. By all accounts, the murderer then sharpened the crease on his pants and slid his head into the noose. It would take fifteen minutes for him to die.

The house on Meadow Pond Road, which George Metalious called Grace's "little dream house on the hill,"[69] is not the home H. H. Holmes was raised in. But it had been the Mudgett family home for many years before Holmes came along and ruined the family name. Just before Herman Mudgett had left for medical school a cousin had drowned there, mysteriously, in the small pond directly across the street from the house. Some believe this cousin, as well as a young playmate of Mudgett's who fell to his death while the two boys explored an abandoned barn, were the first two victims of a burgeoning serial killer.

People in Gilmanton said that the spirit of this cousin still roamed the rooms of the Meadow Pond Road home. That this forlorn spirit haunted the halls because no justice had ever been dealt over their murder at the hands of their cousin Herman. It was one of the reasons why the home had remained empty for so long. Grace didn't mind the thought of a few ghosts at all. If anything, she was looking forward to having the anecdote to share when talking to others.

When Grace decided to buy the home on Meadow Pond Road, she had already spent her $1,500 book advance on bathing suits for hers and the Wilkens kids and put money down on a secondhand Cadillac. She tried to use her book contract as collateral for a loan to buy the Mudgett house, but the bank wouldn't accept it. After offering to sell them *Peyton Place* outright the bank realized she was serious and arranged a mortgage, leaving her novel still in her control. She bought the haunted home with the serial killer connection for $5,000. When the *Peyton Place* royalties finally started to pour in she would put another $100,000 into remodeling it.

The rest of Gilmanton would have been happier had she had just left town altogether. The press got just as much milage out of her tumultuous relations with her Gilmanton neighbors as they did out of the saucier aspects of her books. As far away as California a newspaper would crow that the "new lady author who has made a peep show out of the American small town says she will not move out of her own village come hell, high water, or stares that cut dead."[70] They quoted Grace as saying, "I am not going to move. They can tar and feather me, but I'll not move." Because, if it couldn't be told from the care she used in crafting the little fictional world of Peyton Place, Grace loved Gilmanton. "I really love it here," she finally admitted to an interviewer. "This is home."[71]

Many Gilmanton residents were convinced that the characters of *Peyton Place* were really very thinly veiled versions of themselves. Jeanne Gallant, an early friend of Grace's, said, "They all thought the book was about them. Well, as Grace said, their lives were worse than anything she put in the book."[72]

Laurie Wilkens' son John put more of the blame on the book using the Roberts' crime as the foundation for its story than on its more salacious details. Many of the same people who rallied behind Barbara Roberts after the truth of her upbringing came out were the same people that could not forgive Grace for telling the world about it.

"Because the book was a fictionalized account of an actual local event and the families still were in the area, the town treated her extremely poorly," he said. "They never even put a copy in the town library until Barbara Walters gave Sybil Bryant, a local official, a copy on a live broadcast of the *Today Show.*"[73]

This echoes remarks made by William Dunn, who was chairman of the school board that decided not to renew George Metalious' contract when *Peyton Place* was released. In an interview with some members of the press who had flocked to Gilmanton Dunn said, "It sounded to me. From what I was told, that she is opening up some old wounds in Gilmanton, and I'm afraid there will be some trouble."[74]

The owner of the Gilmanton Corners General Store, Fred Bucciarelli had a similar feeling.

"From what I heard, it's going to hurt a lot of people." He said, explaining that his store would never carry the book. "I'm darned if I'm going to take sides on a story that has split this town in half."[75]

Even if the press, or the nation as a whole, wasn't interested in the true crime roots of *Peyton Place* local folks knew all about it without even needing to be told. Just as the fictional residents, in their way, rallied behind Selena Cross people in the Lake's Region had felt the same about the Roberts. At the height of *Peyton Place's* popularity, Billy Roberts would write a threatening letter to Grace Metalious over her inclusion of their family incident in her novel. Grace took the letter in stride, asking friends if they thought he would bury her body in a sheep pen. Metalious family friends did not find the letter, or the other threatening phone calls she received at 2 a.m. telling her to move, as funny as she had.

Billy Roberts would not be the only person to call Grace Metalious out for cutting a little too close to home. When asked if any other parts of *Peyton Place* were based on real people or events the author would dismiss the question, replying curtly "I hope I have more imagination than that."[76] Nonetheless, Grace would face a lawsuit from a former teacher friend of her husband, Tom Makris, and his wife Geraldine. In the early editions of her book the sexy aggressive new school principal shared the same name as this family friend. Some people have said that the real Tom Makris, a longtime Laconia resident who also closely matched the physical description for the character in the book, was flattered to have a literary namesake. But when the talk began of a *Peyton Place* movie Tom and his wife Geri decided they did not enjoy Grace helping herself to his name for her racy novel. Geri also maintained that the Constance MacKenzie character was based on her life prior to marrying Makris. They sued Grace for libel, asking for a total of $250,000 in damages in two separate lawsuits, saying the tie to the novel had "brought them public hatred, contempt, ridicule, slander, and disgrace."[77] Grace told *Cosmopolitan* magazine that the character name had nothing to do with the teacher she knew personally. She claimed to have been inspired by a restaurant of the same name that she drove past on her way to meet her publisher, The Makris Diner located just outside of Hartford, Connecticut. A release form bearing the Tom Makris signature was also briefly mentioned but never produced. Lawyers for the Makris couple named twenty-eight instances where lines from the book about the character Makris closely matched the real-life Laconia man and his wife. Five days before the trial was slated to be heard it was settled out of court for an estimated $60,000 with Grace and her publishers agreeing to stop using the name. Later editions of the book, its sequel, the movie, and the TV show renamed this character Mike Rossi as a result of that lawsuit.

When the press descended on the small town of Gilmanton it did nothing to endear Grace to the residents. Everyone was convinced that *Peyton Place* was, in some way autobiographical no matter how often Grace pointed back to the murder of Sylvester Roberts. In the same way everyone was just as sure that Gilmanton was really *Peyton Place*. When 20th Century Fox wanted to film part of the *Peyton Place* movie there Gilmanton balked. They wanted nothing more to do with Grace's book than what they felt had already been forced upon them. The nearby city of Laconia felt different. At one point the Chamber of Commerce even sent a telegram to Grace urging her to do whatever she could to convince Hollywood to film in the 'City on the Lakes.'

The truth was, even though the movie studio paid for Grace and her children to spend several weeks in California, they had no interest in where the author thought the movie should be filmed or in what she thought of their changes to her story. Ultimately many of the movie's scenes would be shot in the picturesque town of Camden, Maine. The people of Camden welcomed the media attention and the Hollywood stars who would bring to life the characters Grace had created. Their only disappointment was that Lana Turner would shoot all her scenes back home in California.

When the movie premiered it did so in the Camden Theater, with much fanfare. Bette Davis came with her husband. There were some notable absences that evening though. Lana Turner was still a no-show. The movie studio had offered to pay twenty-five Gilmanton residents for the weekend away to attend the premier, but in the end only thirteen of them would take them up on the offer. Missing too was Grace Metalious. She said she had not been invited.

Chapter Twenty-Three

What day is it when you wake up and realize that what you have is not what you want at all?
— Grace Metalious

Ultimately, ironically even, in many ways Barbara Roberts had a happier ending than Grace Metalious did. In December of 1948, after three weeks of meetings with the state's executive council and just barely a year into Barbara's sentence, Charles Dale, the Granite State's sixty-sixth Governor, pardoned her. He said it was in the "girl's best interests."78 Barbara may have been convicted but she still had people who continued to fight for her. Governor Dale said he had learned of her plight after her family and friends had submitted a petition asking for her release.

Barbara quietly left the Vermont Prison a week before the press would even get wind of her good fortune. The pardon happened so suddenly and unexpectedly that Charles Roberts first heard of it when he called the prison to speak to his sister and was told she had just left. Women's prison Superintendent Helen Koltonski told the bewildered Merchant Marine that a New Hampshire State Trooper and Donald Matson, who was an aide of Governor Dale's, had picked his sister up with no fanfare and given her a ride home. Donald Matson's wife also made the trip to act as a female chaperone to the suddenly free young woman. Koltonski asked Charles for a forwarding address to send

Barbara's belongings to, as the girl had left the prison with so little warning that she didn't even have time to pack a bag. At the end of the month *The Portsmouth Herald* would, in their big end-of-year wrap-up, include the pardoning of Barbara Roberts as "one of the top human-interest stories of the year."[79]

Barbara's family had packed up their things quickly at the end of the trial and left the Gilmanton Iron Works farm where the body of Sylvester Roberts had lain for nine months. The house was closed up until the time came that Barbara and Billy would be free to return to it. Charles and Robert returned to their duties as Merchant Marines. Marjorie and Paul bought a house of their own and moved their small family away from the town where they had spent most of their lives. When Barbara left prison, the family was as supportive as they had been throughout her trial. Billy was returned from The Golden Rule Farm and, when they decided they did not want to return to the family farm where so many bad memories resided, family took the both of them in. Barbara wouldn't live in Gilmanton again, but she stayed in the area. In time her last name changed when she married the boyfriend who had stood by her throughout her confession and incarceration, further obscuring her ties to the crime.

A year after Barbara's pardon by Governor Dale the new Governor of New Hampshire, Sherman Adams, would pardon Billy after a brief closed-door hearing. The boy, who had just turned, 18 wanted to join the Navy and his probation was standing in the way.

More importantly, the press who had salivated over the "girl slayer" quickly lost interest in the story after the announcement of her pardon. Barbara was finally able to lead a normal life. When she passed away on February 7, 2016, in Rochester, New Hampshire, she was a widow, a mother, a grandmother, and a great grandmother. In death she went full circle. Having spent the early part of her life in the unincorporated town of Gilmanton Iron Works, in death she was buried in another unincorporated community, Barnstead Parade, located within the town of Barnstead. She was interred in a small cemetery. It is filled with stones engraved with those fine New England names you see everywhere in old graveyards, Beebes and Nutters, an entire crayon box of colors, Gray, Brown, White. It is the family cemetery of her husband's people. Her gravestone reads "Pure Courage. May She Rest in Peace."

After the publication of *Peyton Place* Grace Metalious would never again have the kind of quiet family life that Barbara Roberts had finally found. The novel brought her fame, a sort of infamy really, and a fortune. Those things brought the kinds of hangers-on that often show up when someone has had a sudden stroke of good fortune such as a large inheritance or winning the lottery. The little girl who had wanted everything and wanted it all the time, the girl who was married and tied down with children while still a teenager, suddenly had money and free time and lots of new friends who wanted her to share both with them. A party began that never really slowed down or ended. Shortly after the book's publication Grace and George divorced. She did not so much lose custody of her children as they simply decided to move in with their father, so they could have regular lives like children should. As part of the divorce settlement Grace agreed to pay for George's college tuition. George agreed to destroy a roll of film he had taken proving that Grace had cheated on him while they were still legally married.

Grace took up with a local man from Laconia named Thomas James Martin, more popularly known as T.J the D.J. thanks to his daily radio show. T.J. was no Tom Makris (or Mike Rossi for fans of the movies and television series) and Grace was no Constance. T.J. and Grace would eventually marry for short time but there was no happily ever after for the *Peyton Place* author. The two brought out the worst in each other; their fights were legendary. Together they lived larger than life. If Grace rented a room at the Plaza, T.J. encouraged her to rent an entire floor. During one epic battle the author threw a mink stole that T.J. had bought for her using her own money out a hotel window. The money Grace earned from the best-selling book in history, and the movie and the television show it inspired, didn't last nearly as long as it should have. Grace drank and partied it all away.

In a short while T.J. and Grace divorced. He had decided enough was enough, that the drinking and partying and fighting had gotten out of hand even for him. Grace said he had tried to pressure her into putting her beloved house on Meadow Pond Road in his name. In 1960 Grace reunited with George and, together, they bought a hotel. Grace was no dummy. She named it the Peyton Place Motel, thinking the name would capitalize on all the publicity generated by her books and movies. But as a marketing ploy the name was a failure; families wouldn't stay there, and Grace went deep into debt renovating the small cabins. The venture couldn't produce enough funds to fuel the lifestyle she had gotten used to. The hotel went under and she and George divorced for a second time. The relationship that had begun as a friendship back when she was a little girl in Manchester was done, this time for good.

Through it all, every time the money started to run out, Grace would put out another book. First, in 1959, there came a sequel to her debut best-seller called *Return to Peyton Place*. It started as just a quick twenty-five-page synopsis for the movie studios to turn into a script. Grace hated the idea but needed the money. Then she agreed to turn that synopsis into a full-length novel when Dell offered her $165,000 for it. The dirty secret of that book was that Grace only managed 98 pages, disjointed and unfinished, which then had to be rewritten and completed by a ghost writer. A movie was also made of that book. This time one of Grace's contractual demands was that it premier at the Colonial

Theater in Laconia and not off somewhere in Maine. It did, but the only celebrity that attended the opening night was Grace Metalious. She was so disappointed; she went home to cry. *Return to Peyton Place* was followed by the book *The Tight White Collar* in 1960 and then *No Adam in Eden* in 1963. Critics who wrote for such laudable venues as *The New York Times Book Review* and *The Chicago Tribune* had, back in the day, found some pretty positive things to say about *Peyton Place*, even when they acknowledged some of its downfalls. Metalious' other books did not fare so well, either with the critics or her readers. The books did well enough sales-wise by any measure other than the one *Peyton Place* had set for them. None of them came anywhere close to the impossibly high bar that first book had set.

In October of 1963, the British journalist John Rees traveled to Gilmanton to interview Grace. A few weeks later he moved in with her at the Meadow Pond Roadhouse. Rees didn't get along with her children and he soon started acting as a go-between with them and their mother. Every time they called, he made an excuse why she couldn't talk. Grace became more and more isolated from her family. John was with her when she fell ill in Boston and had to be rushed to Beth Israel Hospital. No one in her family was told she was there. There was no one to intercede when lawyers arrived to rewrite Grace's will. Everything was left to Rees. Grace made no provisions for her children because, as the will would state, she had "every confidence" that Rees would provide for them if they needed it. Just two hours after signing everything away to a man she had met four months before, Grace died of cirrhosis of the liver brought about from years of drinking. She is supposed to have warned, from her deathbed, to be careful what you wish for, because you just may get it.

The date was February 25, 1964, and she was just 39 years old. Her children would learn of her death the same way the rest of the country did when they saw on the nightly news that New Hampshire's Pandora in blue jeans had died. A lawyer would take up their inheritance case against Rees. During the resulting media free for all it would be discovered that Rees, who called Grace his fiancée, was already married to a woman back home in England with whom he had five kids. He gave up control of the Metalious estate but in the end it was all for nothing. Grace had died with $41,174 in the bank and almost $200,000 worth of debt. The desk, table, and typewriter that Grace had written all her novels on were auctioned off by her family. The winning bid came in at just $75.

In the deathbed will Grace had signed at the hospital, she donated her eyes to Boston's eye bank, with a later clause directing what she wanted done with the rest of her body. "I direct that no funeral services be held for me, and that my body be given the Dartmouth School of Medicine, for the purpose of experimentation in the interest of medical science. If Dartmouth does not accept then to Harvard Medical School."[80] Both Dartmouth and Harvard declined the gift. Still George, representing their three children, had to petition the court for the right to bury Grace in a small, simple ceremony in the Smith Meeting House Cemetery plot she had bought years earlier for herself. Grace's body would be held at the Wilkinson-Beane Funeral Home throughout the court battle and then through the spring of 1964, waiting for the ground to thaw enough for burial. It was the same funeral home, with the addition of a new partner, that had held onto the bones of Sylvester Roberts through the fall and winter of 1947, waiting for the trial of his daughter to conclude and for the family to lay claim to the body.

In one of the final and most lasting insults to Grace Metalious, long after her death, rumors around Gilmanton would persist that she was not even the author of the book they all hated her for writing. Many thought a woman, even one they saw as coarse and uncouth, could never have written such a scandalous book. They believed that George

Metalious had written it and that Grace had taken credit as a type of marketing ploy. This rumor was perpetrated by George himself when he would write his tell-all book, *The Girl from Peyton Place,* in 1965. In this book George presents the idea of writing a novel together as his own, a little project he came up with to keep his wife occupied. George said when he presented the idea to Grace she was excited.

"Oh yes, let's, Gee-Gee," she is supposed to have said when he told her he would help her with the novel as she had a complete disregard for story organization or punctuation. "I could write a wonderful story and maybe this time we could get it published. But what will we write about?"

He generously quotes Grace throughout *The Girl from Peyton Place* as calling the bestselling book "theirs" on multiple occasions. George maintained that he gave full writing credit of *Peyton Place* to Grace to help his wife find herself— and because he did not think a publisher would be interested in the novel if they knew it was a husband-and-wife collaboration. It is worth noting that George Metalious had never mentioned any of these claims while Grace was still alive. No one who knew the couple could ever provide any anecdotes to back up George's stories of co-authorship.

Some believed that Laurie Wilkins was the true author of *Peyton Place*. Laurie had already proven her writing chops with her years of work at *The Laconia Evening Citizen*. Also in her favor, as many saw it, was her college education. Otto Friedrich, the critic and historian, wrote of Grace after her death saying, "The middle-class book reviewers on the middle-class newspapers could have forgiven her such literary sins if she had just gone to college and become a lady."[81] Laurie Wilkins was just this kind of lady, with her college degree from Bernard, her New York pedigree, and the large well-kept farmhouse. Class privilege protected Laurie Wilkens as the supposed author of the "sexsational" novel in a way that Grace would never have been protected.

In her short and troubled life, the former mill worker from humble beginnings had penned a shocking best-selling novel that would then be turned into a slightly more sanitized movie. That movie would then be turned into an even more sanitized television show. The *Peyton Place* television series was a prime-time soap opera that aired two to three times a week for five years on ABC. It starred Mia Farrow as Allison MacKenzie and Ryan O'Neal as bad boy Rodney Harrington. The Cross family, the literary stand-ins for the Roberts, were eliminated as characters in the show from the start. It would surely have upset Grace Metalious, but she died six months before the show ever aired. As the stories of Peyton Place, through movies and years of T.V., became copies of copies of copies, the women behind the book, Grace Metalious and Barbara Roberts, became more and more removed from the story.

Conclusion

It could be any of hundreds of small towns. It isn't one that exists.
— Grace Metalious

I started off this book making what many would consider unlikely comparisons between Grace Metalious, Truman Capote, and Vladimir Nabokov. Few consider *Lolita* or *Peyton Place,* even tangentially, as true crime novels. Many literary theorists have included *Peyton Place* in the "revolt from the village" movement, lumping Metalious in with such greats as Sherwood Anderson and Sinclair Lewis. Purists would say *Peyton Place* is more of a "post-revolt" story as the movement is most often said to of thrived from 1915 to the 1930s. Village revolt writers, to steal a phrase from many of Grace Metalious' reviewers, "blew the lid" off small-town life. They rejected the idea that cities were hotbeds of corruption and or danger while the rural American small town was filled with conservative people with only wholesome values.

But when I look at the life and times of Grace Metalious, the writers I first think of are Sylvia Plath and Shirley Jackson. All three ladies were, as I like to say of myself, New Englanders at heart. Their lives and writing all overlapped the same time period, the early 1950s to early 1960s. Most importantly all three were, as Grace might have said, women who wanted everything and wanted it all the time. It was not that they rejected the ideals of the perfectly put together, loving, capable wife and mother. They wanted to be all that and also so much more. The three shared motherhood, supporting their husbands sometimes to their own detriment, and the drive to write big works that would make those around them question their success at those traditional domestic arts they strived to master. It was not that the three writers were "revolting from the kitchen," but rather it was a case of them hauling a great big typewriter to the middle of the kitchen table and trying to get dinner on the same table for their husbands while pounding away at the keys. It's a dynamic many women struggle with today; under the norms of their times, it was almost guaranteed they could not achieve both. In *Life Among the Savages*, what Shirley Jackson sometimes described as "a disrespectful biography of my children," the author joked about how hard it was to be taken seriously as both a woman and a writer. Jackson painted the scene of showing up at the hospital, in full and active labor with her third child, and being asked to fill out paperwork: "Occupation?" the hospital clerk asks. "Writer," Jackson says. "Housewife," the clerk offers. "Writer," Jackson says. "I'll just put down housewife," the clerk tells her.

There is no indication that I'm aware of that Metalious, Jackson, or Plath were particular fans of each other's work. I suspect that Sylvia Plath probably did not read *Peyton Place* when it was released. In 1956 Plath was studying at Newnham College, one of the women-only schools at the University of Cambridge, on a Fulbright Scholarship. She had just met Ted Hughes and was in the midst of a steamy and passionate courtship with the man she would later marry and have two children with. *Peyton Place* would not even arrive in England's bookstores until a year later. It's only a guess on my part, but I believe that Plath, looking to shed her past writing for glossy women's magazines like *Seventeen* and *Mademoiselle* and be seen as a serious poet, would have avoided the saucy little novel by the housewife from Gilmanton, New Hampshire.

By the time *Peyton Place* was published, Shirley Jackson's most controversial work, *The Lottery*, had already made her a literary landmark. I find it likely that Jackson, married to a literary critic who taught at Vermont's Bennington College and who was a regular entertainer to the staff and students at that university, would have read the book that everyone was talking about. Jackson and her husband read just about everything. Estimates are that their rambling Vermont home contained over 25,000 books. Although known for her wit and sometimes caustic observations, Shirley Jackson was also in many ways the prim and proper wife. I think chances are good that she owned a copy of *Peyton Place,* but it may have been tucked under the mattress, even if only to keep her four children from stumbling across what was written in its pages.

"She was always writing," her oldest son Laurence would say of Jackson. "Or thinking about writing, and she did all the shopping and cooking, too. The meals were always on time."[82]

It should be noted that Jackson, like Grace, also found inspiration in the crimes of the small town she lived in. Her second novel, 1951's *Hangsaman*, was promoted by the publisher as being loosely based on the real-life 1946 disappearance of Paula Jean Welden, a sophomore at Bennington College where Jackson's husband was a professor. In her book *Life Among the Savages*, Jackson would make clear the competing dynamics between domesticity and the darker things in life when she wrote, "I took my coffee into the dining room and settled down with the morning paper. A woman in New York had had twins in a taxi. A woman in Ohio had just had her seventeenth child. A twelve-year-old girl in Mexico had given birth to a thirteen-pound boy. The lead article on the woman's page was about how to adjust the older child to the new baby. I finally found an account of an axe murder on page seventeen and held my coffee cup up to my face to see if the steam might revive me."[83]

Metalious, Plath, and Jackson: all married to teachers and all three would, at various times, express their dislike of fulfilling the responsibilities that the role of the "faculty wife" imposed on them. All three of the writers suffered for their writing. All three felt they had failed at being the type of women society thought they should be. Plath's husband would leave her for one of his mistresses. Plath woke at dawn to write poems before her kids got up and the demands of motherhood took up the rest of her day. Shirley Jackson was racked with anxiety for most of her life and felt compelled to accept her husband's insistence on an open marriage she did not want. Grace was married three times, twice to the same man, and barely saw her own children the last year of her life. When an interviewer asked how she possibly found time to write an entire novel while being a mother to three children Grace replied, "I just made time. And on this basis, I became known as a freak in Gilmanton. Instead of keeping the kids' faces clean I was pounding a typewriter."[84] She said it jauntily enough but deep down the admission cost her. Nobody asked George Metalious how he found time to teach with three kids at home, just like no one asked Ted Hughes or Jackson's husband Stanley Hyman how they found time to write.

All three of these dynamic female voices would die tragically— and well before their times. First went Sylvia Plath in 1963, aged 30. The poet committed suicide after locking her children in a room with bread and milk to hold them over until someone else could discover her body. Then went Grace Metalious in 1964, aged 39, after drinking away her health and her fortune. Shirley Jackson died of a heart attack in 1965 at the age of 48. Feeling ostracized by her neighbors and hating her role as a faculty wife, in the last years of her life she had become increasingly agoraphobic and suffered greater and greater health ailments. Her heart condition was probably exacerbated by her routine use of prescription barbiturates and amphetamines, taken to aid in weight loss and to combat her extreme anxiety.

There were differences between them all, of course. Jackson and Plath, although both felt they were not taken as seriously as writers as their husbands were, both held the sort of college degrees that Grace had believed would have made her more legitimate in the eyes of her detractors. Plath and Jackson were both a part of the art and literary communities of the day, though much of that connection came about because of their writer-professor husbands. Grace had no such creative community to turn to when she struggled. By chance she met W. Somerset Maugham, probably her favorite author, one day in passing at her publisher's offices and it made her as giddy as a schoolgirl. A chance encounter with Orson Welles did not go so smoothly. Grace sent a note saying she'd like to meet him when she noticed he was at a nearby table, dining at the same New York restaurant as she was. Welles, in full view of Grace, crumpled the note in his hand and tossed it away. Shirley Jackson and Sylvia Plath intermingled with almost all the famous literary folk of the day. Grace Metalious had just a typewriter in a corner of the kitchen. At the very end though, really, that is all any of them had. Sylvia at dawn drafting the poems that would make her name after she died, Shirley surrounded by the books she authored that continue to entertain to this day.

Time has been, in many ways, much kinder to Sylvia Plath and Shirley Jackson than it has been to Grace Metalious. A number of books and films have been released in recent years about Plath and Jackson— not just their works, but their lives, their legacies. Grace's life and works have not been given the same treatment. *Peyton Place* went out of print for several years. When Emily Toth was given a grant in 1981 to write a biography of Grace Metalious a colleague at the college she taught at told her "Congratulations on getting money for trash."[85] In 2006 entertainment magazines announced that Sandra Bullock would produce a biopic movie called *Grace*, based on Emily Toth's *Inside Peyton Place* biography from 1981. Sandra Bullock would also play the Grace Metalious role in the movie, with the screenplay being written by Naomi Forner. But the movie never appeared, and no reason was given for it not being released. The Gilmanton Historical Society has featured information on the town's ties to serial killer Herman Mudgett, but they have done nothing of the kind for Grace Metalious, even during the 50th anniversary of the publication of *Peyton Place*.

Sometimes the noise around something— a person, an event, or even sometimes a book, becomes so loud that it drowns out the sound of everything else that it comes near. The uproar over how many Gilmanton residents felt about *Peyton Place* obscured just how much many people loved Grace. When I contacted John Wilkins to see what he might remember of the years the author spent in his mother's kitchen he told me he was happy to help— "so long as there was no smear of her." He told me, "There is much to the story of Grace that is not widely known. Her kindness, generosity, and sense of humor, to name just three."[86]

Along the same vein, while Grace Metalious never hid the truthful origins of her fictional novel, the furor the book raised seemed to bury that fact that there were very real people at the center of it. People who lived very real lives, and oftentimes suffered.

Many readers have focused on the idea that *Peyton Place* reveals the dark secrets hidden behind small-town smiles. I would go a step further and say that the true lesson of Grace's novel, and the real events surrounding Barbara and Sylvester Roberts, is that sometimes the villain and the victim are not as clear cut as it seems at first glance. People also say that *Peyton Place* is a book about female desire, and I agree wholeheartedly! But I'm not talking about the sex. I'm thinking about the desires of Grace Metalious who wanted to write and not have to suffer the sideways glances of her Gilmanton neighbors. I'm also thinking about Barbara Roberts. I think about the girl in the tailored little black dress, chain-smoking with Hollywood flair. The woman she created for herself was so different than the girl who was stuck on the farm, wiping her brother's nose and slaughtering the sheep for years, and dreading when her father might come home.

The world has, in many ways, moved on from *Peyton Place.* While the book's title is still used today to talk about scandals and secrets, many use the phrase without knowing its origins. Ardis Cameron writes, in the introduction to the newest editions of the book, "Even today, the title denotes for most Americans less a particular book than a general set of behaviors, so that *Peyton Place* has become the nation's yardstick against which to measure sexual intrigue and social scandal." While working on this book several people said, "How do I know that name?" or "Oh, that was a book?" when I mentioned my latest project was about *Peyton Place.* The best reaction I got was from two librarians who cackled wildly when they saw me reading my battered, heavily creased, paperback copy at The Fruitland's Museum.

"Is that still in print?" they asked me excitedly. "Oh, we should make that our next book club book. Let's see who we can stir up!"

Delighted librarians aside, overall, the world has moved on. And moved on in ways that seem more like a science fiction novel than anything that would have been written by Grace Metalious! I found myself working on this book during the year we all lost to COVID. Like everything else my yearly mediation retreat had been canceled but I had a friend who knew of a secluded cabin near the ocean where we could hide from the world and be mindful. Dutifully I checked what the current guidelines in New Hampshire were. And then I checked those in Maine. As best I could tell, between both states, I could make the trip and not put myself or anyone else in any extra danger.

I packed my little Mini Cooper convertible, white now, the red one I drove when I first visited Grace Metalious' grave having been traded in. I made sure to bring extra food with me so I wouldn't have to grocery shop once I got to my destination. The weather was not nearly as fine as it was for that backroads adventure through Gilmanton a few years before. Gray and drizzly, the convertible top stayed up. The cabin was a renovated little bungalow from the 1950s and, as promised, I was able to spend a glorious time there without seeing another person. It was the closest thing to normal I had felt in what seemed like a very long time.

The cabin was located just outside of Camden, Maine. The poor weather broke the day I left and after some internal back and forth I decided it was okay if I drove through the center of town on my way out. I wanted to see what places I would recognize from the *Peyton Place* movie. I was amazed at how many tourists still wandered in and out of the charming little downtown shops even in the midst of a pandemic. Yes, I recognized the irony of it, me being a tourist myself, and being surprised that other people from "away" had decided to make the trip.

After cruising the main road, I took a right onto Mechanic Street, the little side street where the Camden Theater was located. When this theater premiered the *Peyton Place* movie on December 11, 1957, it brought in a reported one thousand two hundred visitors and had been used to raise money for the Camden Community Hospital Building Fund. The quaint brick movie theater where Bette Davis saw the movie for the first time is now a flea market-style antique shop. It is the kind of place Laurette De Repentigny would have gone to get a deal on more faux family heirlooms. The movie screen has been removed; the velvet curtain long gone. With every seat pulled from its place the space is now a cavernous white room that has been hastily sectioned off into cubicles where various vendors pile old books and costume jewelry. The marquee that once declared in bold black letters that it was showing the world premiere of *Peyton Place* is also gone, though the structure that held it remains. Now it holds a simple sign that says the name of the shop and its address.

I had been in before, years earlier, in a time when I knew very little about Grace Metalious and never could have guessed I'd one day dedicate a block of my own life to writing a book about her book. Seeing the shop was empty of customers I put on my mask and furtively slipped my camera into my purse. Inside was as I remembered, even now that I was looking at it through the lens of knowing its place in *Peyton Place* history. I did a quick lap through, feeling like I was doing something I should not be. As I walked out the front door, I saw something I had not noticed on any previous trips there. There was an old *Peyton Place* movie poster tucked in one corner, probably around the same place where the wall that had once separated the lobby from the theater had stood. Overlaid on top of an artist's rendition of the typical New England village was a series of almost comic book-style panels. Each one had a different little illustration with a different declaration like "Peyton Place will never forget the day Selena told everything!" or "Peyton Place will never forget the day Lucas returned from the war!"

Two women stood behind a checkout counter. One noticed me looking at the poster and said, "Do you know they filmed that movie here?"

"Oh?" I said, wondering if I felt up to explaining I was writing a book about it, as her fellow employee gave her an almost comically startled look.

"They did?" this second woman inquired, drawing the word out until it had two or three syllables. She looked star-struck.

Her co-worker rolled her eyes and looked at me conspiratorially.

"She's new," she said exasperatedly. "She doesn't know anything. Camden is the *real* Peyton Place."

I didn't correct her. I could have told her that, in addition to Camden, movie scenes were also shot in other Maine towns like Belfast, Whitehall, Mirror Lake, Thomaston, and Rockland and in New York near Lake Placid. All of Lana Turner's scenes were filmed on a set built in Burbank, California. I didn't see any reason at all to tell her that the *real* Peyton Place only ever existed in a made-up spot in the mind of Grace Metalious. It was fiction, interspersed with a couple of more or less true things that happened once in the small town in New Hampshire where the author had lived her short and tragic adult life.

None of it had ever been about any bad feelings particular to Gilmanton, New Hampshire. Grace had picked the name Peyton Place because, to her, it sounded like it could be a small town anywhere. Peyton Place, New Hampshire. Peyton Place, Maine. It made no difference, and it wasn't worth trying to explain to a shop owner in Camden. I felt like Grace would have approved of my decision. Her first thought had always been about what the best story would be. Grace let the facts come second. True life may have inspired many of the tales she spun but those tales were, in the end, her own creations. Peyton Place may never forget, and many in Gilmanton may still remember, but the rest of the world has tucked the Roberts family and Grace Metalious' controversial best-seller into the forgotten corner of urban legend and myth.

Acknowledgments

Writing a book is a tough enough endeavor even in the best of times. In the midst of a pandemic, it becomes nearly impossible. Librarians across New England were kind enough to make me copies of all manner of materials, and email JPGs to me when their branches were closed. Others chose to be flexible about or turn a blind eye to my flagrant disregard of their "One visit per day, one hour per visit" policies when the branches were open. There are people who say that the internet has made libraries, and librarians, obsolete. It must be sad to be so wrong. Not everything can be found on the internet and the job of the librarian is tougher and even more important because of it.

Readers believe that authors create books. Authors know better. Books are never created by just one person. Many of them begin, as this one did, with a publisher who takes a chance on some wacky idea a writer has. I have now written a number of books on a number of different topics but I never fail to feel a giddy sense of joy when a publisher takes that chance on me. Behind every author is a team of editors and designers. As always, they get the credit for everything that was done well, and I take the blame for anything I got wrong.

The latter part of writing a book, at least for me, involves a certain selfish single-mindedness. In this case my headspace was so filled with the past I might as well have been a time traveler from the 1940s or 50s. While my friends talked current events, I mentioned something I had read that day in a newspaper from 1947 or shared an advertisement from the 1950s I thought seemed funny. My housekeeping may have reached Metalious level lows. As always, much love to the friends and family who tolerate me during these times. My children have told me that the only thing harder than writing a book is living with someone who is writing a book, and I suspect they might be right.

Photos

Gilmanton has no monuments or plaques for Grace Metalious or Peyton Place but in 2015 the city of Manchester changed the name of a previously unnamed alley near Pearl and Bridge Streets to "Grace Metalious Lane."

The former L.W. Packard Wool Mill where Barbara Roberts confessed to her brother Charles that she had murdered their father nearly a year previously.

The rest of the complex that made up the LW. Packard Wool Mill

The Laconia Tavern Inn where Grace liked to regale friends and fans with wild tales

The Laconia Tavern Inn, which once saw visitors like Grace Metalious and President Eisenhower, is now subsidized housing.

Like many writers, Grace Metalious loved the library. But she hated the architecture of Laconia's Gale Memorial Library. The author would drink at the bar across the street and make up jokes for the other patrons about how awful she thought it looked.

The courthouse where the trial of Barbara and Billy Roberts took place. Today it is used as the offices for Belknap County.

The employee entrance of Manchester's Amoskeag Mill where Grace Metalious worked before becoming an author. Photo Courtesy of the Library of Congress.

Barbara and Billy Roberts on the day of their arraignment.

An advertisement for the Peyton Place movie

The premier of the Peyton Place movie would take place in Camden Maine, where several exterior scenes were shot. Grace would insist that the sequel premier here at the Colonial Theater in Laconia, New Hampshire. The author cried after attending the Laconia premier because no Hollywood celebrities were in attendance.

Grace used her Peyton Place royalties to buy her dream home, the family home of a historical serial killer. Today the home is the Gilmanton Winery. While much has been made of the animosity between Grace Metalious and the other residents of Gilmanton the current owners of the Gilmanton Winery are proud of its literary roots.

The black iron gates to Smith Meeting House Cemetery where Grace Metalious is buried

Fans of Peyton Place and writers still leave offerings on Grace Metalious's grave, more than fifty years after her death

A simple stone for a complicated woman. It sits far apart from the rest of the cemetery's dead, as Grace wanted.

The Camden Theater where the Peyton Place movie had its world-wide premier is now an antique store

The Camden Public Library is home to the Peyton Place archives, focusing mostly on the movie and not the novel.

These vintage postcards show the town centers of Gilmanton Iron Works, where the Roberts murder took place, and of Camden Maine where the Peyton Place movie was filmed.

Bibliography

"Barbara and Billie to Enter Pleas" *The Laconia Evening Citizen* (Laconia, New Hampshire) November 1, 1947

"Barbara's Fan Mail Heavy: Girl Held for Murder, Now in Concord, Cheered by Messages" *The Laconia Evening Citizen* (Laconia, New Hampshire) September 25, 1947

"Barbara Reported Sane by Tests" *The Laconia Evening Citizen* (Laconia, New Hampshire) October 7, 1947

"Barbara Smiles for First Time" *The Laconia Evening Citizen* (Laconia, New Hampshire) September 9, 1947

"Barbara Taken to Concord" *The Laconia Evening Citizen* (Laconia, New Hampshire) September 23, 1947

"Barbara Taken to State Prison" *The Laconia Evening Citizen* (Laconia, New Hampshire) December 2, 1947

"Barbara Takes News Calmly" *The Laconia Evening Citizen* (Laconia, New Hampshire) October 29, 1947

"Barbara Wept Often on Job: Fellow Employees at Packard Mill Thought Girl Nervous Over Learning to Run Machine" *The Laconia Evening Citizen* (Laconia, New Hampshire) September 11, 1947

Barnicle, Peter. "Peyton Place Revisited" *The Boston Sunday Herald* (Boston, Massachusetts) January 16, 1966

"Battered Body Found in Grass Along Merrimack River Bank" *The Lowell Sun* (Lowell, Massachusetts) *September* 8, 1947

"Brother and Sister Indicted for Second Degree Murder" *The Laconia Evening Citizen* (Laconia, New Hampshire) October 29, 1947

Callahan, Michael. "Peyton Place's Real Victim" *Vanity Fair (*New York, New York) January 22, 2007.

Cameron, Ardis. *Unbuttoning America: A Biography of "Peyton Place"* Ithaca; London: Cornell University Press, 2015.

Caruchet, Matthew. "'A Christmas Carol' Sending the Poor to Prison" Economic Opportunity Institute December 22, 2018

"Counsel Confers with Barbara" *The Laconia Evening Citizen* (Laconia, New Hampshire) September 10, 1947

Creadick, Anna G. "The Erasure of Grace: Reconnecting "Peyton Place" to Its Author." *Mosaic: An Interdisciplinary Critical Journal* 42, no. 4 (2009)

Crossman, Paul. "Rutland Historical Society Quarterly" Vol. 30, No. 1, 2000

Davis, Chester. "Defends Sister who Slew Dad: Corroborates Tragic Story Behind Death" *The New Hampshire Sunday News* (Manchester, New Hampshire) September 7, 1947

"December 1 Set as Date for Murder Trial" *Laconia Evening Citizen* (Laconia, New Hampshire) October 30, 1947

"Door of Roberts Kitchen Taken to State Police Office in Concord" *Laconia Evening Citizen* (Laconia, New Hampshire) September 8, 1947

Eaton, Aurore. *The Amoskeag Manufacturing Company: A History of Enterprise on the Merrimack River.* Charleston, South Carolina: The History Press, 2015.

Eddy, Cheryl. "This Scandalous 1946 Small Town Murder Helped Inspire *Peyton Place*" Gizmodo.com July 28, 2015.

"F. E. Normandin to Defend Barbara" *Laconia Evening Citizen* (Laconia, New Hampshire) September 9, 1947

Flint, Justin. "'Once Upon a Time' Becomes True Story: Homeless Boys Learn that Happiness is Real at Golden Rule Farm" *The Portsmouth Herald* (Portsmouth, New Hampshire) December 11, 1940

Friedrich, Otto "Farewell to Payton Place" *Esquire* December 1971

"Full Pardon Given Barbara Roberts, Confessed Slayer" *The Portsmouth Herald* (Portsmouth, New Hampshire) December 21, 1948

Gallagher, Justin F. "Roberts Girl Collapses in Prison Cell" *The New Hampshire Sunday News* (Manchester, New Hampshire) December 7, 1947

"Gilmanton Girl Confesses Shooting Father Last Christmas" *The Laconia Evening Citizen.* (Laconia, New Hampshire) September 6, 1947

"Girl, 20, Held in Yuletide Murder of Father: Body was Buried in Sheep Pen" *The Daily Times* (Davenport, Iowa) September 6, 1947

“Girl Prisoner Is Pardoned” *Rutland Daily Herald* (Rutland, Vermont) December 22, 1948

“Girl Slayer Pardoned: Barbara Roberts, 22, Released from Vermont Prison” *Barre Daily Times* (Barre, Vermont) December 21, 1948

“Grace Metalious Is Dead at 39; Author of ‘Peyton Place’ Novel; Writer Shocked the Nation with the Story of Lurid Life in New England Town” *The New York Times* (New York, New York) Feb. 26, 1964

Howe, Amasa “Girl, Brother Plead Guilty in N.H. Slaying: Pair Sentenced for Manslaughter in Father’s Death” *The Boston Globe* (Boston, Massachusetts) December 3, 1947

“Iron Works Chief Able to Testify” *Laconia Evening Citizen.* (Laconia, New Hampshire) November 3, 1947

Italie, Hillel “Scandalized N.H. Town Revisted by ‘Peyton’ Past” *The Washington Post.* (Washington, D.C.) March 12, 2006

Janson, Ebba M. “Barbara, Quiet Black-Clad Girl of 20, Tells Where She Dragged Dad’s Body” *The Laconia Evening Citizen.* (Laconia, New Hampshire) September 6, 1947

Janson, Ebba M. “Clue Furnished Brothers by Uncle Known as Boy Orator of England” *The Laconia Evening Citizen.* (Laconia, New Hampshire) September 6, 1947

Janson, Ebba M. “Trial Gets Under Way After Visit by Jury to Gilmanton” *The Laconia Evening Citizen* (Laconia, New Hampshire) December 2, 1947

“Judge Grimes Opens Session” *The Laconia Evening Citizen.* (Laconia, New Hampshire) October 28, 1947

“Judge Tempers Dad Killers’ Sentences: Barbara Roberts and Brother Plead Guilty.” *The Lowell Sun* (Lowell, Massachusetts) December 3, 1947

“Jury Chosen in Roberts Murder Trial: Two Charged with Father’s Slaying” *The Lowell Sun.* (Lowell, Massachusetts) December 2, 1947

Kadpal, Disha. “Where Was Peyton Place Filmed?” RepublicWorld August 14, 2020

Keller, Julia. “Scandal! Outrage!” *The Chicago Tribune* (Chicago, Illinois) July 23, 2006.

Kelly, George. “50 Shades of Grace: The Impact of Peyton Place on New Hampshire Sixty Years Later” New Hampshire Magazine. March 1, 2013

Kenney, Michael. “Once Racy, Now Passe, ‘Peyton Place’ Makes a Comeback” *The Boston Globe.* (Boston, Massachusetts) April 29, 1999.

“Laconia Girl Worries About Brother as She Starts Sentence” *Lewiston Evening Journal* (Lewiston, Maine) December 3, 1947

“Laconia, N.H. Girl Pleads Not Guilty to Murder of Father: Confession Tells How Slayer Lived in Fear of Parent” *The Lowell Sun.* (Lowell, Massachusetts) September 6, 1947.

“Laconia Girl Tells How She Murdered Her Father.” *The Lowell Sun, evening edition.* (Lowell, Massachusetts) September 6, 1947.

“’Lady-Like’ Girl Held in Death of Sailor-Father Months Ago” *The Atlanta Constitution* (Atlanta, Georgia) September 7, 1947

“Legal Conference Delays Start of Trial” *The Nashua Telegraph.* (Nashua, New Hampshire) December 1, 1947

McManus, Tony. “Historically Speaking: A Look at Dover’s Legal History, Courts and Jurists” *Foster’s Daily Democrat,* (Dover, New Hampshire) March 31, 2019

“Medical Expert to Go Over Bones” *Laconia Evening Citizen.* (Laconia, New Hampshire) September 6, 1947

Metalious, George and O’Shea, June. *“The Girl from Peyton Place”* New York, New York: Dell Publishing, 1965

Metalious, Grace “Me and Peyton Place” *American Weekly* (New York, New York) June 1, 1958

Metalious, Grace “Why I Returned to my Husband.” *American Weekly* (New York, New York) January 29, 1961

“Metalious Heir Renounces Claim” *The Fresno Bee* (Fresno, California) March 2, 1964

“Mill Worker Begins Prison Term” *The Newport Daily Express.* (Newport, Vermont) December 3, 1947

“Mother Held in Murder of Baby Girl” *The Lowell Sun* (Lowell, Massachusetts) December 3, 1947

“Murder Trial will Open Monday” *The Laconia Evening Citizen.* (Laconia, New Hampshire) November 29, 1947

“Peyton Place Author Named in Two Suits” *The Bangor Daily News* (Bangor, Maine) March 15, 1957

“Peyton Place Author Sued for $250,000” *The Boston Globe* (Boston, Massachusetts) March 15, 1957

“’Peyton Place’ Lawsuit Settled” *St. Joseph News Press* (St. Joseph, Missouri) November 27, 1958

“Politics, Industrial Exodus Lead N.H.’s Big ’48 News” *The Portsmouth Herald* (Portsmouth, New Hampshire) December 31, 1948.

“Pound Guilty of Assault and Battery” *The Lowell Sun* (Lowell, Massachusetts) September 6, 1947

Quigg, H. D. “New Small Town ‘Peep Show’ Lady Author Snubbed by Neighbors Now” *The Desert Sun* (Palm Springs, California) October 3, 1956

“Rumors of ‘Spicy’ Book Split New Hampshire Town Even Before Printing” *The Sacramento Bee* (Sacramento, California) August 30, 1956

“Shocker Novel About N.H Town Makes Author Social Outcast” *The Ogden Standard Examiner.* (Ogden, Utah) October 2, 1957.

“Slaying of Sylvester Roberts Exposed, 2 Man Hunts Here” *The New Hampshire Sunday News*. (Manchester, New Hampshire) September 14, 1947

Smith, Raymond. “Barbara Hunted Chief Night She Killed Dad” *Laconia Evening Citizen* (Laconia, New Hampshire) September 12, 1947

Smith, Raymond. “Family Behind Barbara and Billy to Limit Says Brother Charlie” *Laconia Evening Citizen.* November 3, 1947

“Together Again at Arraignment” *Laconia Evening Citizen* (Laconia, New Hampshire) November 4, 1947

Toth, Emily. *Inside Peyton Place: The Life of Grace Metalious.* Jackson, Mississippi: University Press of Mississippi, 1981.

“Town in Uproar Over Earthy Novel About New England Life” *The Bennington Banner* (Bennington, Vermont) August 29, 1956

“Trial of Barbara and Billy Opens After Long Conference with Judge” *The Laconia Evening Citizen.* (Laconia, New Hampshire) December 1, 1947

“Two Guns in Murder at Gilmanton: Police Say Girl’s Story of Slaying Dad Shows Discrepancies.” *The Lowell Sun.* (Lowell, Massachusetts) September 8, 1947

United States of America, Bureau of the Census. *Sixteenth Census of the United States, 1940*. Washington, D.C.: National Archives and Records Administration, 1940. T627, 4,643 rolls.

Wade, Alan. "Jury Views Scene of N.H. 1946 Yuletide Slaying: Pretty Woolen Mill Worker and Schoolboy Brother Charged with Murdering Their Dad" *The Lowell Sun* (Lowell, Massachusetts) December 2, 1947

Warn, Emily. "Poetry Meets Peyton Place" *Seattle Weekly* (Seattle, Washington) October 9, 2006

Weinman, Sarah. *The Real Lolita: The Kidnapping of Sally Horner and the Novel that Scandalized the World.* New York, New York: Harper Collins Publishers, 2018.

"William Roberts, 16, in Court in Connection with Murder" *Laconia Evening Citizen*. (Laconia, New Hampshire) September 9, 1947

"William Roberts Pardoned in Fathers Death" *The Nashua Telegraph.* (Nashua, New Hampshire) April 28, 1949

"Woman Prisoner in Daring Jail Break" *The Nashua Telegraph*. (Nashua, New Hampshire) June 5, 1947

Works Cited

Introduction

1 Edmund Fuller. Best Seller Revisited: Return to Peyton Place. *The New York Times* November 29,1959

2 Sarah Weinman. *The Real Lolita: The Kidnapping of Sally Horner and the Novel that Scandalized the World.* New York, New York: Harper Collins Publishers, 2018.

3 Sarah Weinman. *The Real Lolita: The Kidnapping of Sally Horner and the Novel that Scandalized the World.* New York, New York: Harper Collins Publishers, 2018. Pg. 5

Chapter One

4 Emily Toth. *Inside Peyton Place: The Life of Grace Metalious.* Jackson, Mississippi: University Press of Mississippi, 1981. Pg. 8

5 George Metalious and June O'Shea. "*The Girl from Peyton Place*" New York, New York: Dell Publishing, 1965. Pg. 13

6 George Metalious and June O'Shea. "*The Girl from Peyton Place*" New York, New York: Dell Publishing, 1965

7 George Metalious and June O'Shea. "*The Girl from Peyton Place*" New York, New York: Dell Publishing, 1965.

Chapter Two

8 Grace Metalious "Me and Peyton Place" American Weekly, June 1, 1958. Pg. 11

9 Grace Metalious "Why I Returned to my Husband." *American Weekly* January 29, 1961

Chapter Three

10 Emily Toth. *Inside Peyton Place: The Life of Grace Metalious.* Jackson, Mississippi: University Press of Mississippi, 1981. Pg. 78

11 Emily Toth. *Inside Peyton Place: The Life of Grace Metalious.* Jackson, Mississippi: University Press of Mississippi, 1981. Pg. 79

12 In an email to the author

Chapter Four

13 Chester Davis "Defends Sister who Slew Dad: Corroborates Tragic Story Behind Death" *The New Hampshire Sunday News.* September 7, 1947

Chapter Five

14 "Barbara Hunted Chief Night She Killed Dad" *Laconia Evening Citizen* September 12, 1947

15 Ebba M. Janson "Barbara, Quiet Black-Clad Girl of 20, Tells Where She Dragged Dad's Body" *The Laconia Evening Citizen.* September 6, 1947

Chapter Seven

16 Ebba M. Janson "Barbara, Quiet Black-Clad Girl of 20, Tells Where She Dragged Dad's Body" *The Laconia Evening Citizen.* September 6, 1947

Chapter Eight

17 As reprinted in "Laconia, N.H. Girl Pleads Not Guilty to Murder of Father: Confession Tells How Slayer Lived in Fear of Parent" *The Lowell Sun.* September 6, 1947.

18 "Laconia, N.H. Girl Pleads Not Guilty to Murder of Father: Confession Tells How Slayer Lived in Fear of Parent" *The Lowell Sun.* September 6, 1947.

19 "Laconia, N.H. Girl Pleads Not Guilty to Murder of Father: Confession Tells How Slayer Lived in Fear of Parent" *The Lowell Sun.* September 6, 1947.

20 "Laconia Girl Tells How She Murdered Her Father." *The Lowell Sun, evening edition.* September 6, 1947.

Chapter Nine

21 Ebba M. Jenson "Barbara, Quiet Black-Clad Girl of 20, Tells Where She Dragged Dad's Body" *The Laconia Evening Citizen.* September 6, 1947

22 "Laconia, N.H. Girl Pleads Not Guilty to Murder of Father: Confession Tells How Slayer Lived in Fear of Parent" *The Lowell Sun.* September 6, 1947.

Chapter Ten

23 "Fined $30 for Assault on Woman" The Lowell Sun, September 8, 1947

24 "Mother Held in Murder of Baby Girl: Alleged Killer Says Crime Took Place in 1945" The Lowell Sun, December 3, 1947

25 "Man is Captured with Girl Kidnap Victim in Detroit" Davenport, Iowa: The Daily Times, September 6, 1947 and "Abducted Girl Safe After Six-Hour Ride" The Atlanta Constitution, September 7, 1947

26 "Battered Body Found in Grass Along Merrimack River Bank" The Lowell Sun, September 8, 1947

27 "Confession Tells How Slayer Lived in Fear of Parent" The Lowell Sun, September 6, 1947

28 "Girl Prisoner Is Pardoned" Rutland Daily Herald December 22, 1948

29 "Full Pardon Given Barbara Roberts, Confessed Slayer" *The Portsmouth Herald* December 21, 1948

30 "Laconia Girl Tells How She Murdered Her Father." *The Lowell Sun, evening edition.* September 6, 1947.

31 "Laconia, N.H. Girl Pleads Not Guilty to Murder of Father: Confession Tells How Slayer Lived in Fear of Parent" *The Lowell Sun.* September 6, 1947.

32 Alan Wade. "Jury Views Scene of N.H. 1946 Yuletide Slaying: Pretty Woolen Mill Worker and Schoolboy Brother Charged with Murdering Their Dad" *The Lowell Sun* December 2, 1947

33 "'Lady-Like' Girl Held in Death of Sailor-Father Months Ago" *The Atlanta Constitution* September 7, 1947

34 "Gilmanton Girl Confesses Shooting Father Last Christmas" *The Laconia Evening Citizen*. September 6, 1947

35 Raymond Smith. "Barbara Hunted Chief Night She Killed Dad" *Laconia Evening Citizen* September 12, 1947

36 Chester Davis. "Defends Sister who Slew Dad: Corroborates Tragic Story Behind Death" *The New Hampshire Sunday News*. September 7, 1947

37 "Barbara's Fan Mail Heavy: Girl Held for Murder, Now in Concord, Cheered by Messages" *Laconia Evening Citizen*. September 25, 1947

38 "Teen-Agers, Red-Haired Wife Held for Ambushing Male" The Atlanta Constitution, September 7, 1947

Chapter Eleven

39 "Door of Roberts Kitchen Taken to State Police Office in Concord" *Laconia Evening Citizen*. September 8, 1947

40 Chester Davis. "Defends Sister who Slew Dad: Corroborates Tragic Story Behind Death" *The New Hampshire Sunday News*. September 7, 1947

41 "Door of Roberts Kitchen Taken to State Police Office in Concord" *Laconia Evening Citizen*. September 8, 1947

Chapter Twelve

42 "Barbara's Fan Mail Heavy: Girl Held for Murder, Now in Concord, Cheered by Messages" *Laconia Evening Citizen*. September 25, 1947

Chapter Thirteen

43 "Counsel Confers with Barbara" *The Laconia Evening Citizen*. September 10, 1947

44 "William Roberts, 16, in Court in Connection with Murder" *Laconia Evening Citizen*. September 9, 1947

Chapter Fifteen

45 Raymond Smith. "Barbara Hunted Chief Night She Killed Dad" *Laconia Evening Citizen* September 12, 1947

46 Smith, Raymond. "Barbara Hunted Chief Night She Killed Dad" *Laconia Evening Citizen* September 12, 1947

Chapter Seventeen

47 Ebba M Janson. "Trial Gets Under Way After Visit by Jury to Gilmanton" *The Laconia Evening Citizen* December 2, 1947

Chapter Eighteen

48 Amasa Howe "Girl, Brother Plead Guilty in N.H. Slaying: Pair Sentenced for Manslaughter in Father's Death" *The Boston Globe* December 3, 1947

49 Amasa Howe "Girl, Brother Plead Guilty in N.H. Slaying: Pair Sentenced for Manslaughter in Father's Death" *The Boston Globe* December 3, 1947

50 "Mill Worker Begins Prison Term" The Newport Daily Express. December 3, 1947

51 "Judge Tempers Dad Killers' Sentences: Barbara Roberts and Brother Plead Guilty." *The Lowell Sun* December 3, 1947

52 "Judge Tempers Dad Killers' Sentences: Barbara Roberts and Brother Plead Guilty." *The Lowell Sun* December 3, 1947

53 "Mill Worker Begins Prison Term" The Newport Daily Express. December 3, 1947

54 "Judge Tempers Dad Killers' Sentences: Barbara Roberts and Brother Plead Guilty." *The Lowell Sun* December 3, 1947

55 "Judge Tempers Dad Killers' Sentences: Barbara Roberts and Brother Plead Guilty." *The Lowell Sun* December 3, 1947

Chapter Nineteen

56 Bob Kennedy "Sport City" The Portsmouth Herald October 9, 1947

57 Justin Flint. "'Once Upon a Time' Becomes True Story: Homeless Boys Learn that Happiness is Real at Golden Rule Farm" *The Portsmouth Herald.* December 11, 1940

58 Justin Flint. "'Once Upon a Time' Becomes True Story: Homeless Boys Learn that Happiness is Real at Golden Rule Farm" *The Portsmouth Herald.* December 11, 1940

59 Justin Flint. "'Once Upon a Time' Becomes True Story: Homeless Boys Learn that Happiness is Real at Golden Rule Farm" *The Portsmouth Herald.* December 11, 1940

60 Justin Flint. "'Once Upon a Time' Becomes True Story: Homeless Boys Learn that Happiness is Real at Golden Rule Farm" *The Portsmouth Herald.* December 11, 1940

Chapter Twenty

61 Justin Gallagher. "Roberts Girl Collapses in Cell" *The New Hampshire Sunday News*. December 7, 1947

62 Sarah Cleghorn and Dorothy Canfield. *Miss Ross's Girls Graphic Survey*. August 1, 1931. UVM.edu

63 "Charge Prison Director Overlooked Sex Racket" The Portsmouth Herald January 8, 1949

Chapter Twenty-One

64 George Kelly. "50 Shades of Grace: The Impact of Peyton Place on New Hampshire Sixty Years Later" New Hampshire Magazine. March 1, 2013

65 Toth, Emily. *Inside Peyton Place: The Life of Grace Metalious.* Jackson, Mississippi: University Press of Mississippi, 1981.

66 Michael Callahan. "Peyton Place's Real Victim" *Vanity Fair.* January 22, 2007.

Chapter Twenty-Two

67 Otto Friedrich "Farewell to Payton Place" Esquire December 1971, Pg. 163

68 "Holmes Tells His Story" The Chicago Chronical April 11, 1896

69 George Metalious and June O'Shea. "*The Girl from Peyton Place"* New York, New York: Dell Publishing, 1965

70 H.D Quigg "New Small Town 'Peep Show' Lady Author Snubbed by Neighbors Now" Palm Springs, California: The Desert Sun October 3, 1956

71 H.D Quigg "New Small Town 'Peep Show' Lady Author Snubbed by Neighbors Now" Palm Springs, California: The Desert Sun October 3, 1956

72 Julia Keller. "Scandal! Outrage!" The Chicago Tribune. July 23, 2006.

73 Email to the author

74 "Town in Uproar Over Earthy Novel About New England Life" The Bennington Banner August 29, 1956

75 "Rumors of 'Spicy' Book Split New Hampshire Town Even Before Printing" The Sacramento Bee August 30, 1956

76 During question and answer period after being the luncheon speaker for the Laconia Chamber of Commerce, as quoted in *Inside Peyton Place: The Life of Grace Metalious* by Emily Toth. Jackson, Mississippi: University Press of Mississippi, 1981.

77 Toth, Emily. *Inside Peyton Place: The Life of Grace Metalious.* Jackson, Mississippi: University Press of Mississippi, 1981. Pg. 175

Chapter Twenty-Three

78 "Girl Slayer Pardoned: Barbara Roberts, 22, Released from Vermont Prison" *Barre Daily Times.* December 21, 1948

79 "Politics, Industrial Exodus Lead N.H.'s Big '48 News" The Portsmouth Herald. December 31, 1948.

80 Holland v. Metalious 105 N.H. 290 (1964)

81 Otto Friedrich "Farewell to Payton Place" *Esquire* December 1971

Conclusion

82 Rachel Cooke "Laurence Jackson Hyman on His Mother Shirley: Her Work is so Relevant Now" The Guardian. December 12, 2016

83 Shirley Jackson *Life Among the Savages* New York, New York: Penguin Books, 1953

84 H. D. Quigg. "New Small Town 'Peep Show' Lady Author Snubbed by Neighbors Now" Palm Springs, California: The Desert Sun October 3, 1956

85 Anna G. Creadick. "The Erasure of Grace: Reconnecting "Peyton Place" to Its Author." *Mosaic: An Interdisciplinary Critical Journal* 42, no. 4 (2009)

86 In an email with the author

For More News About Renee Mallett,
Signup For Our Newsletter:
http://wbp.bz/newsletter

Word-of-mouth is critical to an author's long-term success. If you appreciated this book please leave a review on the Amazon sales page:
http://wbp.bz/peytonplacea

AVAILABLE FROM STEVE KOSAREFF AND WILDBLUE PRESS!

SATIN PUMPS by STEVE KOSAREFF

http://wbp.bz/satinpumpsa

Made in the USA
Monee, IL
29 October 2022

16800753R10105